Road Atlas
SOUTH AFRICA

CW00742662

CONTENTS

ATLAS SECTION

TOURIST AREA MAPS

STREET MAPS

STRIP ROUTES

2 ROAD SIGNS

REGULATORY SIGNS

Control signs

 Yield

 One-way roadway

 No entry

Command signs

 Minimum Speed

 Keep left

 Proceed right only

Turn right

 Pay toll

Goods vehicle only

Prohibition signs

 Speed limit

 Left turn ahead prohibited

 Right turn prohibited

 U turn prohibited

 Overtaking prohibited

 Parking prohibited

 Stopping prohibited

 Height limit

 Goods vehicle prohibited

Reservation signs

 Bus lane

 Limited Parking

Comprehensive signs

 Dual carriageway freeway

 Single carriageway freeway

Derestriction signs

 Dual carriageway freeway

Exclusive secondary signs

 Maximum stay during two periods or days time limit

WARNING SIGNS

Road layout signs

 Crossroad

 Skew T-junction

 Side road junction from right

 Staggered junction

 Y-junction

 Sharp junction (to left)

 Two-way traffic

Direction of movement signs

 Traffic circle

 Gentle curve (to right)

 Sharp curve (to left)

 Hairpin bend (to right)

 Concealed driveway (right)

 Combined curves (first to right)

 Two-way traffic crossroad

Symbolic signs

 Left lane ends

 Traffic control "yield" ahead

 End of dual roadway (to right)

 Pedestrian crossing

 Wild animals

 Motor gate (to left)

Railway crossing

 Slow-moving heavy vehicles

 Gravel road begins

 One vehicle-width structure

 Road narrows from one side only (right)

 Slippery road

 Speed humps

 Falling rocks (from right)

 General warning (any type of danger ahead)

 Emergency flashing light

Drift

T-junction

 Traffic signals

 Traffic control "stop" ahead

Hazard marker signs

 Danger plate

 Double railway crossing

Sharp curve chevron (left)

Sharp curve chevron (left)

 T-junction chevron

GUIDANCE SIGNS

Route marker signs

Direction signs

Advance direction sign

Confirmation signs

Location signs

Street names   Provincial borders   Freeway name

Direction sign symbols

Airport

Mine

Alternative route

Toll route

Supplementary plate signs

Police

Tow-away zone

Tourism signs

Race course   Golf course

Scenic route   View point   Waterfall   Hiking trail

General tourist attraction   National monument   Museums   Theatre   Amphitheatre

Accommodation facility   Bed and breakfast   Rooms (bed only)   Caravan site   Camp site

Parking area   Tourist information   Roadside stall/ Curio shop   Shop

Crocodile farm   Bird park/ Sanctuary   Ostrich farm   Ostrich farm   Snake park

Botanical gardens   Wine cellar   Mine museum   Boat launch/ Watersport

Police   Hospital (with name)   SOS call station (for sign)   Telephone

Filling station and workshop   Filling station   Workshop   Tow-in service   Truck services

INFORMATION SIGNS

300m

Cull-de-sac

Right of way

Multi-phase robots

Information centre

Diagrammatic signs

Restriction/prohibition applicable in right lane

Converging of traffic lanes

ROAD SURFACE MARKINGS

Regulatory

Mandatory direction arrows

No crossing

Exclusive parking bay and symbols

No stopping line (certain times)

No parking

Yield line

No overtaking

Warning

Block pedestrian crossing

Railway crossing ahead

Yield sign ahead

Speed hump

No overtaking or no crossing line ahead

Guidance

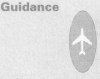
Airport

4 DISTANCE TABLE

	UMTATA	PRETORIA	PORT ELIZABETH	MBABANE	MASERU	MAPUTO	MAFIKENG	KIMBERLEY	JOHANNESBURG	GABORONE	EAST LONDON	DURBAN	CAPE TOWN	BLOEMFONTEIN
BLOEMFONTEIN	570	456	677	677	157	897	464	177	398	622	584	634	1004	•
CAPE TOWN	1314	1460	769	1680	1160	1903	1343	962	1402	1501	1079	1753	•	1004
COLESBERG	517	682	451	903	383	1123	672	292	624	848	488	860	778	226
DURBAN	439	636	984	562	590	633	821	811	578	979	674	•	1753	634
EAST LONDON	235	1040	310	1238	630	1301	1048	780	982	1206	•	674	1079	584
GABORONE	1192	350	1299	719	702	957	158	538	358	•	1206	979	1501	622
GEORGE	880	1229	335	1450	913	1670	1203	762	1171	1361	645	1319	438	773
GRAAFF-REINET	503	880	291	1101	599	1321	854	490	822	1012	395	942	787	424
GRAHAMSTOWN	415	1057	130	1418	692	1478	1065	667	999	1223	180	854	899	601
JOHANNESBURG	869	58	1075	361	438	599	287	472	•	358	982	578	1402	398
KEETMANSHOOP	1547	1354	1431	1657	1283	1895	1072	897	1296	1230	1468	1708	995	1074
KIMBERLEY	747	530	743	833	334	1071	380	•	472	538	780	811	962	177
LADYSMITH	517	414	1062	386	366	567	597	587	356	755	752	248	1413	410
MAFIKENG	1034	294	1141	648	544	886	•	380	287	158	1048	821	1343	464
MAPUTO	1064	583	1609	223	853	•	886	1071	599	957	1301	633	1903	897
MASERU	616	488	822	633	•	853	544	334	438	702	630	590	1160	157
MBABANE	1003	372	1548	•	633	223	648	833	361	719	1238	562	1680	677
MESSINA	1392	461	1594	797	949	725	680	991	519	696	1501	1107	1921	917
NELSPRUIT	976	322	1434	173	713	244	635	827	355	672	1226	707	1762	757
PIETERMARITZBURG	360	557	905	640	511	706	742	732	499	900	595	79	1674	555
PIETERSBURG	1181	250	1383	504	738	605	569	780	308	485	1290	886	1710	706
PORT ELIZABETH	545	1133	•	1548	822	1609	1141	743	1075	1299	310	984	769	677
PRETORIA	928	•	1133	372	488	583	294	530	58	350	1040	636	1460	456
UMTATA	•	928	545	1003	616	1064	1034	747	869	1192	235	439	1314	570
UPINGTON	1047	854	933	1157	731	1395	572	397	796	730	968	1208	894	574
WELKOM	718	316	830	451	249	813	321	294	258	479	737	564	1156	153

Although the greatest care has been taken in compiling the kilometre table and ensuring that the road distances given conform to the latest information available, no responsibility for errors can be accepted by the publishers, who would welcome any suggested amendments. The kilometres indicate the shortest distance between any two places over tarred roads wherever possible.
To find the distance between any two places in the table read down and across the respective connecting columns.
An example is given above in which the distance between Cape Town and Pretoria is shown as 1460 kilometres

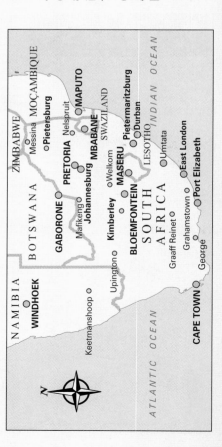

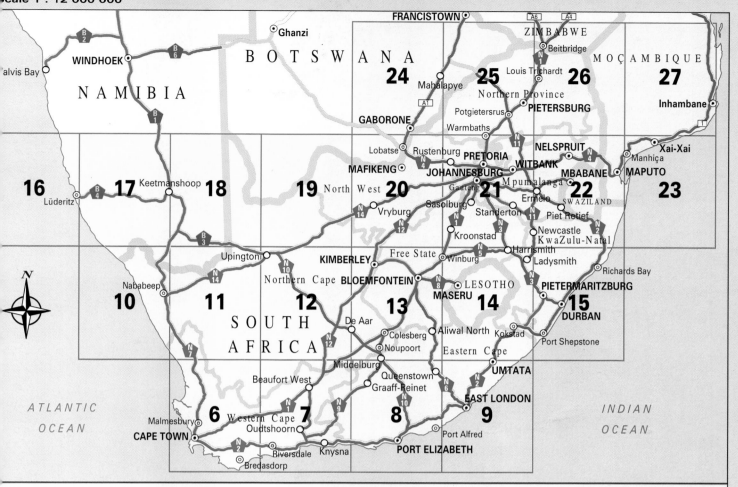

Scale 1 : 12 000 000

LEGEND TO ATLAS SECTION

Scale 1 : 1 500 000

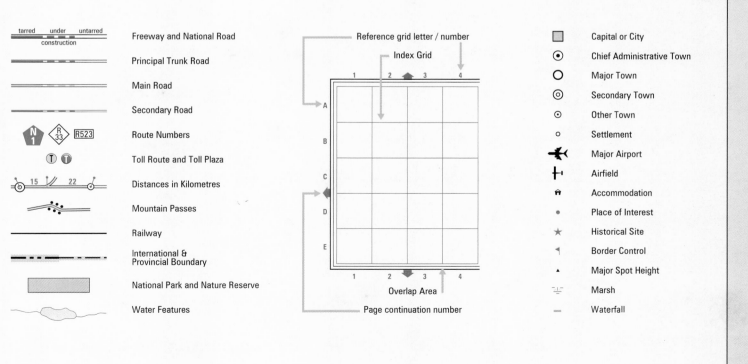

Freeway and National Road	Capital or City
Principal Trunk Road	Chief Administrative Town
Main Road	Major Town
Secondary Road	Secondary Town
Route Numbers	Other Town
Toll Route and Toll Plaza	Settlement
Distances in Kilometres	Major Airport
Mountain Passes	Airfield
Railway	Accommodation
International & Provincial Boundary	Place of Interest
National Park and Nature Reserve	Historical Site
Water Features	Border Control
	Major Spot Height
	Marsh
	Waterfall

Reference grid letter / number
Index Grid
Overlap Area
Page continuation number

Scale 1 : 1 500 0

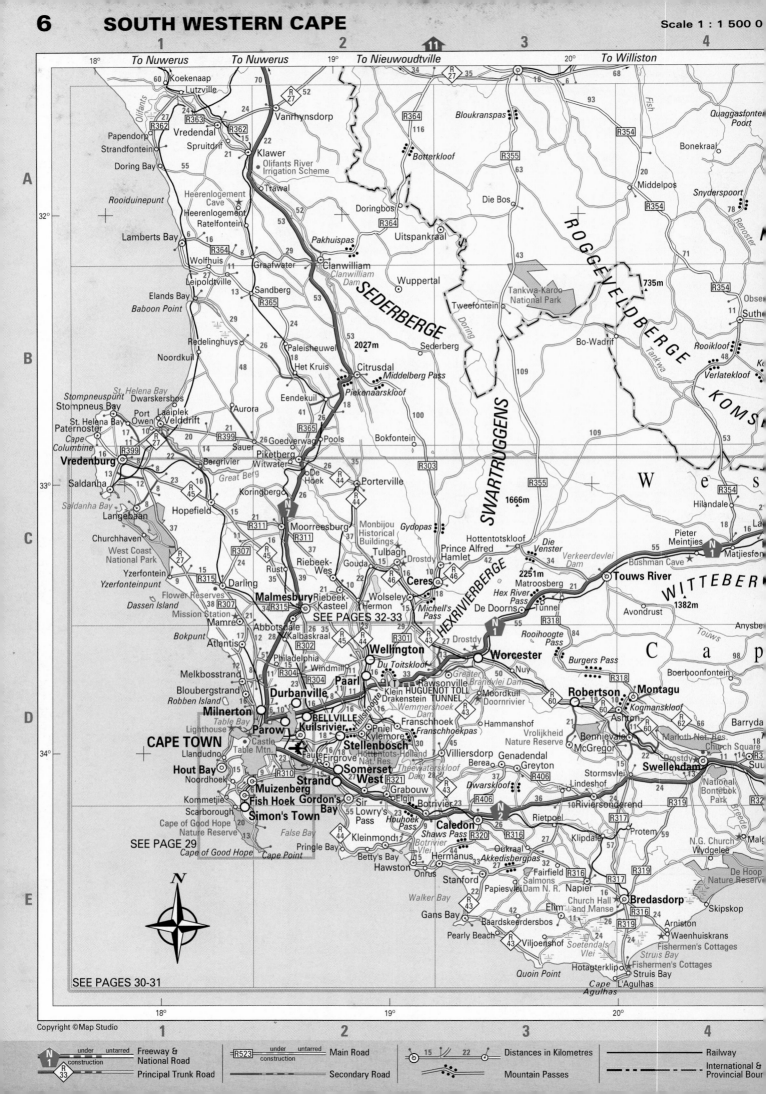

Scale: 5 10 20 30 40 50km

Columns: 5 | 6 | 12 | 7 | 8

Williston — To Carnarvon 22° — To Victoria West 23° — To Richmond 24° — To Graaff-Reinet

Row A

Loxton, Meltonwold, Hutchinson
R356, R381, Verster, R63, Biesiespoort
R308, Saaifontein, Wagenaarskraal, N1
R353, R356, Corbelled House
Fraserburg, R381, Sneeukraal, Three Sisters, Murraysburg
R356, R353, Rosedene, Restvale, R63
93, Rosedene, 89, 32°

Row B

Teekloof Pass, Molteno Pass, Nelsport
Hondefontein, Karoo National Park, 1913m, Renosterkop, Kariega
NUWEVELDBERGE, Rosesberg Pass, Old Town Hall, N.G. Church, R61
Beaufort West, Droërivier, R306, R61, R61
721m, Merweville, Letjiesbos, Wiegnaarspoort, 121
R353, Luttig, Leeugamka Dam, Amos

Row C

ngplaas, Leeu-Gamka, Kaapse Poortjie
Buffels, Kruidfontein, N9, Beervlei Dam
Zwarts, Rietbron, Volstruisleegte, Miller, 1450m
Blockhouse, Prince Albert Road, R407, WITTEBERGE, R306, Perdepoort, R329, R329
N1, Koup, Seekoegat, Kommandokraal, 1414m, Willowmore
Vleifontein, Prince Albert, 2152m, Water Mill, Klaarstroom, BAVIAANSKLOOFBERGE
Floriskraal Dam, Swartberg Pass, GROOT SWARTBERGE, Meiringspoort, Buyspoort, Ghwarriepoort, 1627m, Nuwekloof, Studtis

Row D

Gamkapoort Dam, Cango Caves, De Rust, Olifants, KOUGABERGE
Vleiland, Matjiesrivier, Kruisrivier, Grootkraal, Schoemanspoort, Schoemanshoek, R328, R341, N9, Zaaimansdal
Ladismith, Kraaldorings, Huisrivier Pass, R62, Oudtshoorn, Dysselsdorp, Suspension Bridge, KAMMANASSIEBERGE, Potjiesberg Pass, Uniondale, Uniondale Poort
Calitzdorp, Oosgamo, De Hoop, Koutjie, Buffelsdrif, Daskop, Molenrivier, Avontuur, Misgund, Louterwater
R62, Zoar, Rooiberg Pass, Volmoed, Kamanassie Dam, N12, Montagu Pass and Old Smithy, N9, Noll, Speelmanskraal, De Vlug, 1715m, Joubertina
R327, R323, Van Wyksdorp, OUTENIEKWABERGE, Herold, Outeniqua Pass, Kleinplaat, Prince Alfreds Pass, R339, The Crags, TSITSIKAMMABERGE
Brandrivier, Robinson Pass, Old Tollhouse, Bergplaas, Karatara, R340, Grootrivier Pass, Bloukrans Pass, Stormsrivier
Garcia Pass, Toll House, Cloetes Pass, Blanco, George, Rondevlei, Homtini Pass, Big Tree, Tsitsikamma Nat. Park, TSITSIKAMMA TOLL ROAD
LANGEBERG, Langberg, R327, Ruitersbos, Sinksabrug, Wilderness, Phantom Pass, Witedrift, N2, Paul Sauer Bridge
elberg, Du Plessis Pass, Herbertsdale, Brandwag, Pacaltsdorp, Sedgefield, Knysna, Plettenberg Bay
Riversdale, R328, Herolds Bay, Wilderness National Park, Belvidere Church, Walker Point, The Heads, Knysna National Lake Area, Cape Seal

Row E

N2, Albertinia, R327, Groot Brakrivier, Hartenbos
R305, Droëvlakte, Dana Bay, Vlees Bay
Riethuiskraal, Vermaaklikheid, Johnson's Post, Vlees Bay, Mossel Bay
Still Bay East, Cape Vacca (Kanonpunt), Gouritsmond
Still Bay West, Groot Jongensfontein
Cape Barracouta, Sebastian Bay

SEE PAGES 34-35

INDIAN OCEAN

Bottom columns: 5 | 6 | 7 | 8

21° — 22° — 23° — 24°

Legend:

- ▪ Capital or City
- ▪ Chief Administrative Town
- ● Major Town
- ◉ Secondary Town
- ◎ Other Town
- ○ Settlement
- ✈ Major Airport
- Airfield
- ⌂ Accommodation
- • Place of Interest
- ★ Historical Site
- Border Control
- Ⓣ Toll Route
- Ⓣ Toll Plaza
- ▲ Major Spot Height
- Game & Nature Reserves
- Marsh
- Waterfall

5 10 20 30 40 50km

5 · 6 · 14 · 7 · 8

28° · To Mount Frere 29° · To Lusikisiki · 30°

Indwe · Garryowen · Calapas · Umtata Dam · Nobantu · Rock of Execrution · 31

Cala · Whitmore · Ntibane 61 · UMTATA · 100 Libode · Mlenganapas · Gemvale

R359 · 31 · 45 Satansnek · Langdon · R61 · 61 Misty Mount · 23 Ntshilini · 66 · R61

Askeaton · Lufuta · Engcobo · Coghlan · Buntingville · Old Bunting · Tombo · Port St. Johns

Lady Frere · Tsazo · All Saints Nek · Mgwali · Viedgesville · Ngqeleni · Notintsila · Silaka Nature Reserve

Ncora Dam · Clarkebury · Mqanduli

Southeyville · Nobokwe · Bashee Bridge · Bityi · Ngqungqu · Hluleka Nature Reserve

Qamata · Qombolo · Garner's Drift · Munyu · Elliotdale · Old Morley · Tshani · A

St. Marks · Hange · Coffee Bay · 32°

Lubisi Dam · Cofimvaba · Tsomo · Idutywa · Alderley · Rothmere · Mncwasa Point

Xolobe · Ngamakwe · Ebende · Taleni · Hobeni

1820 Settlers Milestones · Willowvale · Ciko · The Haven

hcart · Butterworth · Nyokana · Dwesa Nature Reserve

Bolo Reserve · Qoboqobo · Manubi · Nqabara

Forest rve · Dohne · Mgwali · Great Kei River Bridge · Cats Pass · Qora Mouth

tterheim · Kei Cuttings · Centani · Mazeppa Bay

Bethel · Komga · Great Kei · B

Grave R352 · Amabele · Mpetu · Wavecrest

mahoek · Kei Road · R349 · Qolora Mouth

Dam · Maclantown · Quko · Kei Mouth

schweig R346 · Bisho · Tainton · Morgan's Bay

Breidbach · Historic Buildings · Haga-Haga

illiams · Berlin · Cintsa

Zwelitsha · Potsdam · Dawn · Gonubie Mouth

Mdantsane · EAST LONDON · Beacon Bay · 33°

Sittingbourne · Bonza Bay · Fort Glamorgan

Chalumna · Kidd's Beach · C

Bell R345 · Hamburg

Wesley

Fish Point

INDIAN OCEAN

SEE PAGES 38-39

D

34°

E

East London coastline

28° · 29° · 30°

5 · 6 · 7 · 8

Copyright © Map Studio

Capital or City	Secondary Town	Major Airport
Chief Administrative Town	Other Town	Airfield
Major Town	Settlement	Accommodation
Place of Interest	Toll Route	Game & Nature Reserves
Historical Site	Toll Plaza	Marsh
Border Control	Major Spot Height	Waterfall

JAKKALSBERGE

Sendelingsdrif

Richtersveld National Park

Khubus

Oranjemund
Alexander Bay

*Border Crossing only
with permit*

To Grünau 18

D316

Orange

Haib

50

B1

Kotzehoop

Noordoewer
Noordoewer

Vioolsdrif

Holgat

Eksteenfontein

74

29°

Lekkersing

Anenous Pass

Steinkopf

B

Port Nolloth
Mc Dougall's Bay

93

R382

N7

Bülletrap

44

Wedge Point

Nigramoep

R355

Nababeep

ATLANTIC OCEAN

Grootmis

Buffels

93

Miners' Memorial
Springbok

Kleinsee

Kommaggas

Melkbospunt

C

30°

Messelpad Pass

Wildeperdehoek Pass

Soebatsfontein

Kamieskr

Skulpfonteinpunt

Koïingnaas

Hondeklipbaai

Spoegrivier

Wallekraal

Karl

Strandfonteinpunt

D

Nariep

Groen

Groenriviersm

Island Point

Kotzesr

31°

E

Augrabies Falls

15°

16°

17°

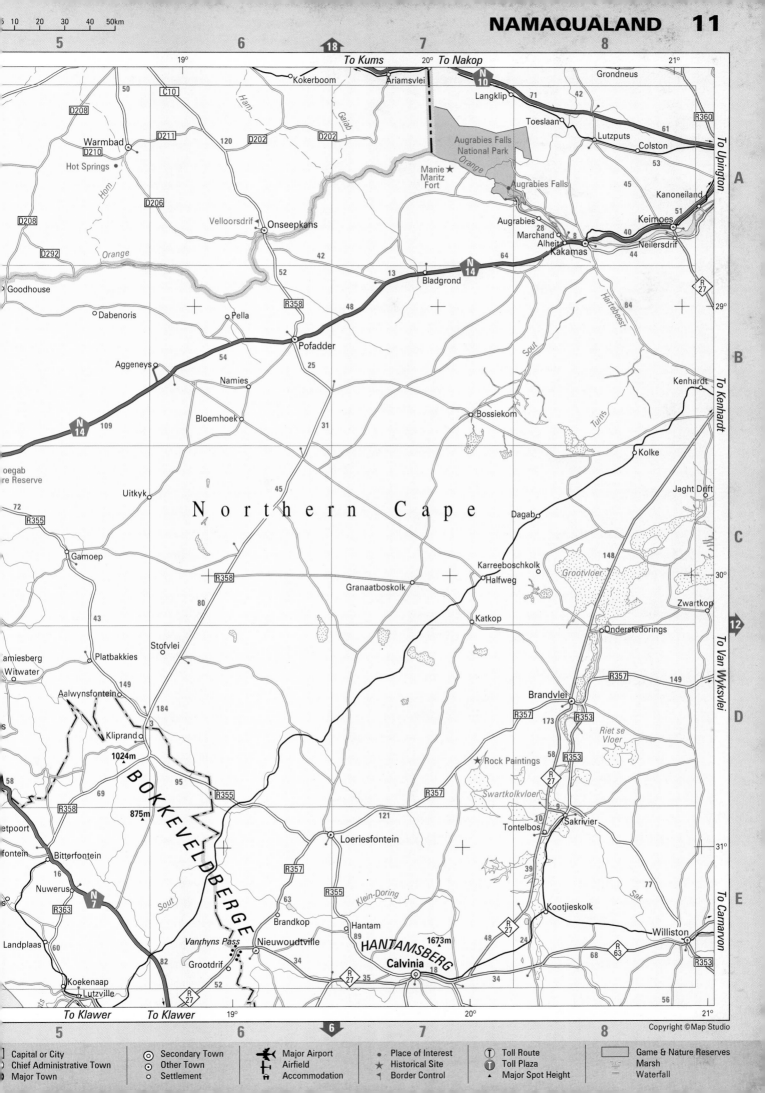

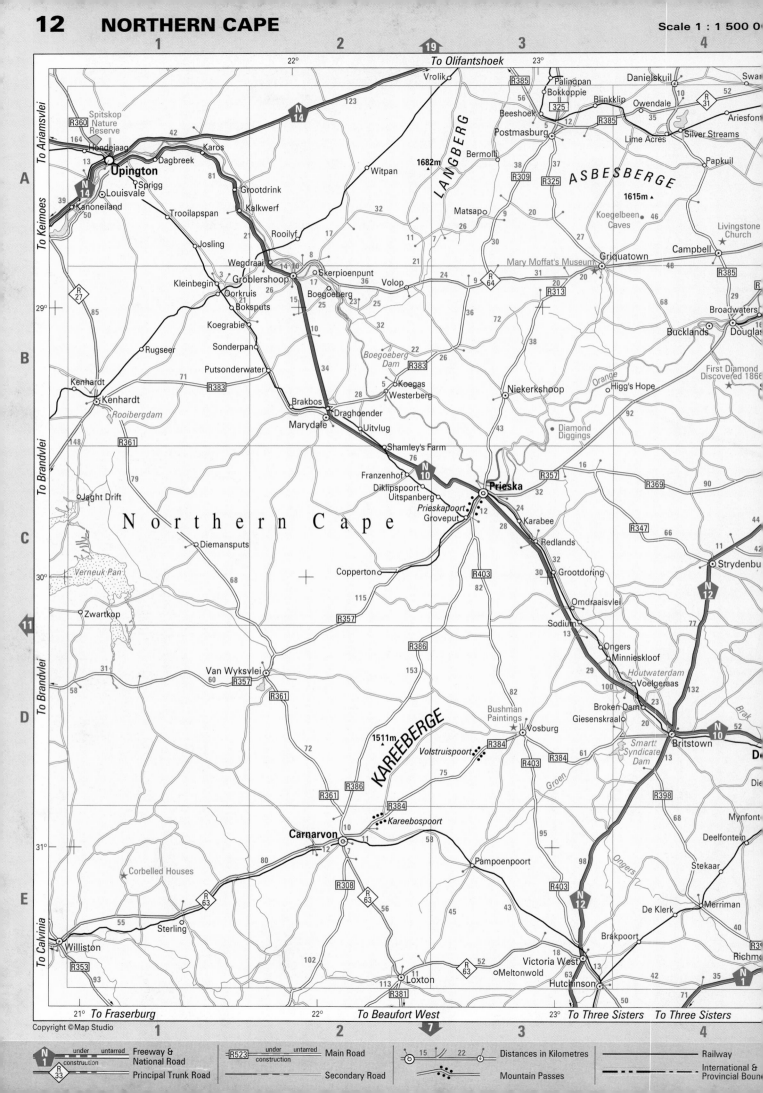

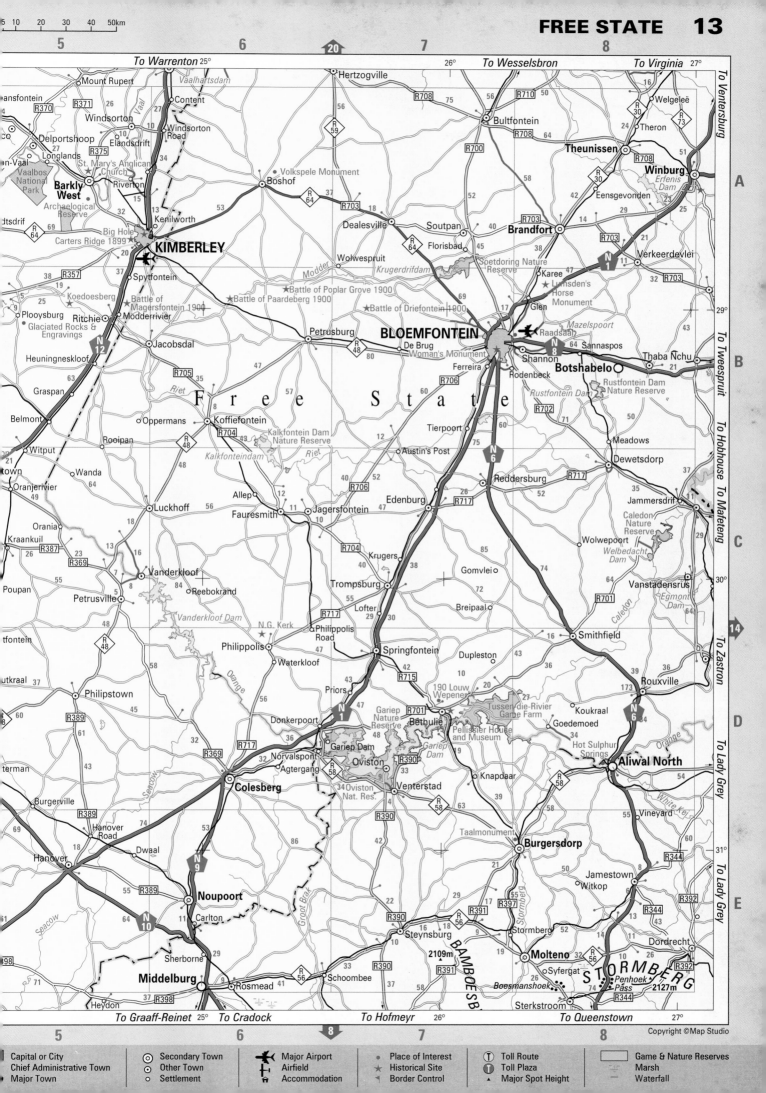

Scale: 5 10 20 30 40 50km

To Vryheid · To Vryheid · To Nongoma · 22

Dundee · Nondweni · Nhlazatshe · Hlabisa · Bushlands · Cape Vidal

Wasbank · Vant's Drift · Nqutu · 85 · 34 · 50 · Mahlabatini · Hluhluwe Umfolozi Park · 80 · N2 · 20

Rorke's Drift · R68 · 29 · Silutshana · Uloliwe · Ilangakazi · Umfolozi Game Reserve · 50 · 26 · Mtubatuba · St. Lucia · Mapelane Nature Reserve

Helpmekaar · Elandskraal · Isandhlwana · Babanango · **Ulundi** · Nodwengu · Ulundi 1879 · Ondini · Umunywana · Mtubatuba · Riverview · Lake Eteza Nature Reserve · Teza

Pomeroy · Mangeni · Dingaan's Kraal · 60 · R68 · Mtonjaneni · 24 · Melmoth · Dondotsha · Kwa Mbonambi · Mposa

KwaZulu - Natal · Qudeni · Nkandla · Randalhurst · 27 · Ndundulu · R34 · 46 · 13 · 10 · Enseleni Nature Reserve

SEE PAGE 90 · Tugela Gorge · Dlolwana · Cetshwayo's Grave · 55 · The Ranch · Nkwalini · 25 · **Empangeni** · Felixton · **Richards Bay**

Tugela Ferry · Ntunjambiti · Entumeni · R66 · Coward's Bush Monument · 32 · 28 · Richards Bay Game Reserve

Keate's Drift · Muden · R74 · Kranskop · Eshowe · Fort Nongqai · Fort Kwa-Mondi · 26 · 18 · Umlalazi Nature Reserve · Mtunzini

R33 · **Greytown** · Ahrens · 39 · R74 · 24 · Battle of Gingindlovu · Amatikulu · **Gingindlovu**

General Louis Botha's Birthplace · KwaSizabantu Mission · Fort Mtombeni · Nyoni · R61 · NORTH COAST TOLL ROAD

R622 · R33 · Mapumulo · 51 · Mandini · R102 · Battle of Tugela 1838

Burn Dam · Rietvlei · Sevenoaks · Otimati · Tugela · Darnall · Tugela Mouth · Fort Pearson · Ultimatum Tree

LANDS TOLL ROUTE · York · Dalton · Fawnleas · 79 · **Stanger** · Shaka's Memorial · Zinkwazi Beach

Kloof Nature Reserve · New Hanover · R614 · Aldinville · Shakaskraal · 18 · Sheffield Beach

Howick · Falls · Albert Falls · Wartburg · Valley of 1000 Hills · Umhlali · Shaka's Rock · Salt Rock

Merrivale · 35 · Queen Elizabeth Park · Ndwedwe · **Tongaat** · Ballito

Hilton · Geloftedam · Colenso Mission Station 1854 · 15 · **NORTH COAST TOLL ROAD** · Newsel and Umdloti Beach

PIETERMARITZBURG · Ashburton · Inanda · Camper- · 27 · **INDIAN OCEAN**

Thornville · 38 · Kranskloof Nature Reserve · Phoenix · Umhlanga

Hammarsdale · **Clermont** · **KwaMashu**

Mpumalanga · 60 · MARIANNHILL TOLL ROAD · **Pinetown** · **DURBAN**

Rosebank · Nshongweni Dam · **Queensburgh** · The Bluff

42 · **Umlazi** · Umbumbulu

Rhodes' House · R603 · **Isipingo**

R56 · Adams Mission · Umbogintwini · **Amanzimtoti**

N2 · **Kingsburgh**

Dududu · Umgababa

PAGES 42-43 · Vernon Crookes Nature Reserve · 28 · **Umkomaas** · Clansthal

R612 · 60 · **Umzinto** · Scottburgh · Park Rynie

Braemar · Kelso · Pennington

37 · Sezela

R102 · Ifafa Beach · Mtwalume · Turton

St. Faith's · Dweshulu · **Hibberdene** · Umzumbe

22 · Southport · Sea Park · Umtentweni

Marburg · **Port Shepstone** · Shelley Beach

R620 · **Uvongo** · **Margate** · **Ramsgate** · Southbroom

Palm Beach · Glenmore Beach · Mvuna Nature Reserve · Port Edward

SEE PAGES 40-41

Mlambonya River in the Northern Drakensberg

Copyright ©Map Studio

● Capital or City	◉ Secondary Town	✈ Major Airport
Chief Administrative Town	◎ Other Town	✈ Airfield
Major Town	○ Settlement	⌂ Accommodation

● Place of Interest	Ⓣ Toll Route
★ Historical Site	Ⓣ Toll Plaza
Border Control	▲ Major Spot Height

Game & Nature Reserves · Marsh · Waterfall

ATLANTIC OCEAN

Franciscus Bay

Oystercliffs ○

Mercury Island ○
Spencer Bay ○

K a r a s

Hottentots Bay

○ Hottentot B

Ichabo Island

Lüderitz Bucht

Lüderitz
Diaz Point
Site of original Diaz Cross
Ghost Mining Tov
Ko

Elizabeth
Possession Isl

Albatros

Pomo

A house in the ghost mining town of Kolmanskop

under   untarred   Freeway &
construction   National Road
R33   Principal Trunk Road

R523   under   untarred   Main Road
construction
Secondary Road

15   22   Distances in Kilometres
Mountain Passes

Railway
International &
Provincial Bou

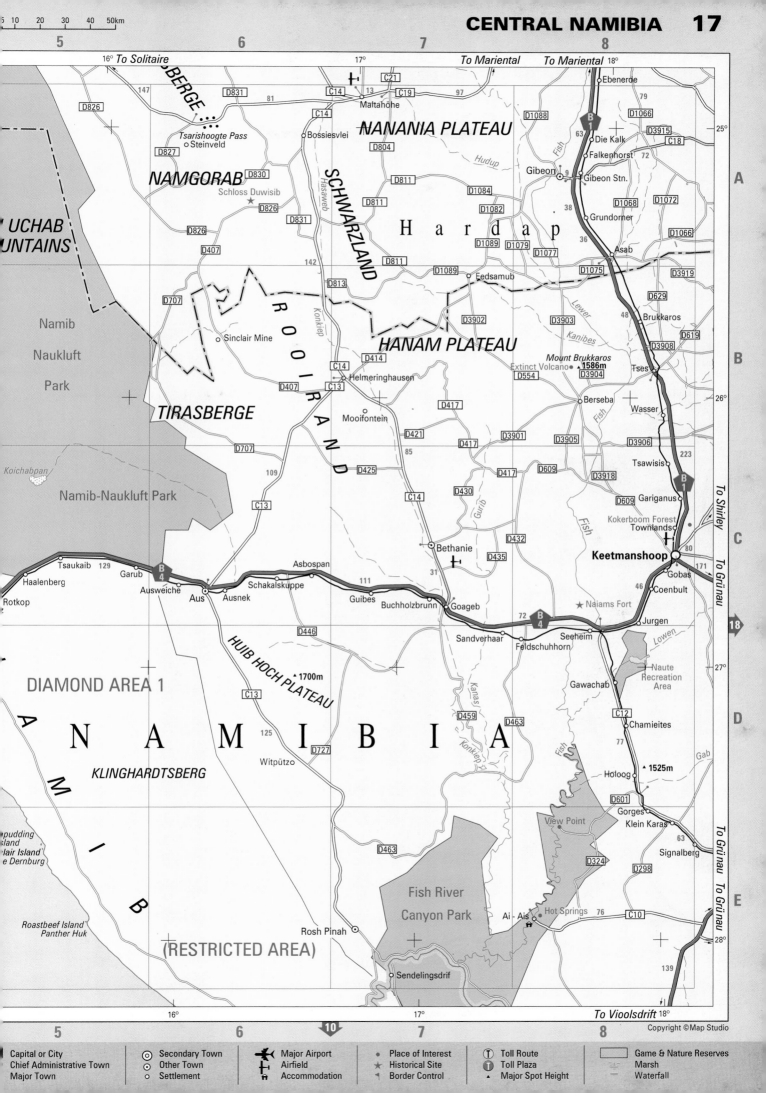

5   10   20   30   40   50km

5   6   7   8

16° To Solitaire   17°   To Mariental   To Mariental 18°

D831   81   C14   13   C21   C19   97   Ebenerde
147   D826   C14   Maltahöhe   D1088   B1   63   Die Kalk   D1066   79   25°
Tsarishoogte Pass   C14   Bossiesvlei   NANANIA PLATEAU   Falkenhorst   D3915   C18
D827   Steinveld   D804   Hudup   Gibeon   9   Gibeon Stn.   72

NAMGORAB   D830   D811   H a r d a p   38   D1068   D1072   A
Schloss Duwisib   D826   D811   D1084   Grundorner   D1066
D831   D407   D811   D1082   36   Asab
142   D811   D1089   D1079   D1075   D3919
D813   D1089   D1077   D629
ROOIRAND   Eedsamub   Lewer   D3908   Brukkaros   B
Sinclair Mine   D3902   D3903   48   D619
D414   HANAM PLATEAU   Kanibes
C14   Mount Brukkaros   D3908
Helmeringhausen   D554   Extinct Volcano   ▲1586m   Tses
D407   C13   D3904
TIRASBERGE   D417   Berseba   Wasser   26°   B
Mooifontein   D3901   D3905   Fish   D3906
D421   D417   Tsawisis   223
D707   85   D425   D417   D609   D3918   B1
C13   D430   D609   Gariganus
C14   Kokerboom Forest
Koichabpan   D432   Townlands   80
Namib-Naukluft Park   109   Bethanie   D435   **Keetmanshoop**   171   C
31   Gobas
Tsaukaib   129   Asbospan   Naiams Fort   46   Coenbult
Haalenberg   Garub   B4   Schakalskuppe   111   72   B4   Jurgen   To Grünau
Rotkop   Ausweiche   Aus   Ausnek   Guibes   Buchholzbrunn   Goageb   Seeheim   Lowen   18°
D446   Sandverhaar   Feldschuhhorn
HUIB HOCH PLATEAU   ▲1700m   Naute Recreation Area   27°
DIAMOND AREA 1   C13   Gawachab   D
N A M I B I A   Kanas   C12   Chamieites
KLINGHARDTSBERG   125   D459   D463   77   Gab
D727   Witpützo   Konkiep   Holoog   ▲1525m
D601
pudding   Gorges
land   D463   View Point   Klein Karas
Dernburg   D324   D298   63   Signalberg   E
Roastbeef Island   Fish River   Ai-Ais   Hot Springs   76   C10
Panther Huk   Canyon Park   28°
Rosh Pinah   139
(RESTRICTED AREA)
Sendelingsdrif   To Vioolsdrift 18°

Capital or City   ◉ Secondary Town   ✈ Major Airport   • Place of Interest   Ⓣ Toll Route   ▭ Game & Nature Reserves
Chief Administrative Town   ◎ Other Town   Airfield   ★ Historical Site   Ⓣ Toll Plaza   Marsh
Major Town   ○ Settlement   ⌂ Accommodation   ◄ Border Control   ▲ Major Spot Height   Waterfall

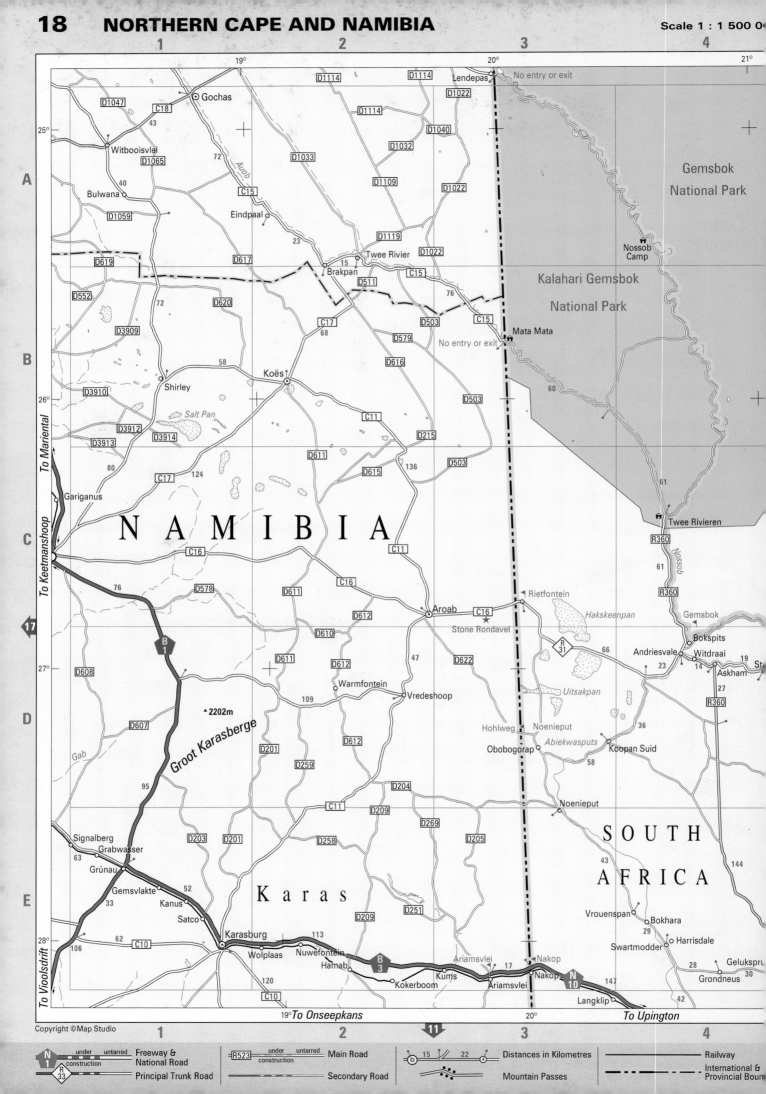

5 10 20 30 40 50km

5   **6**   **7**   **8**

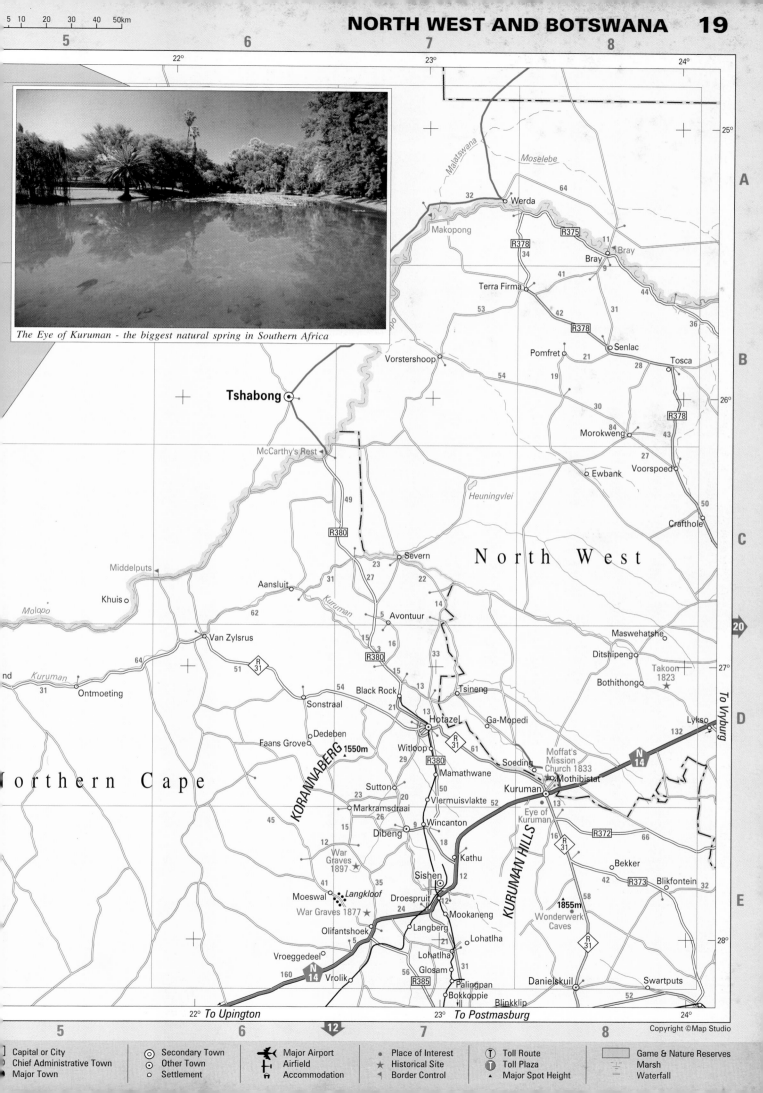

The Eye of Kuruman - the biggest natural spring in Southern Africa

22°

Malatswana

Moselebe

32   Werda   64

Makopong

R378   R375

34   11   Bray

Bray   9

41

Terra Firma

53   42   31   44

R378

Pomfret   21   Senlac

Vorstershoop

54   19   28   Tosca

Tshabong

30   R378

84   Morokweng   43

McCarthy's Rest

27

Ewbank   Voorspoed

49

Heuningvlei

R380

50   Crafthole

Severn   **N o r t h   W e s t**

23

Middelputs

31   27   22

Aansluit

14

Khuis   62   5   Avontuur

Molopo

Maswehatshe

20

Van Zylsrus   15   16   Ditshipeng

64   R31   3   R380   33   Takoon 1823

51   15

Kuruman   Bothithongo

31   Ontmoeting   54   Black Rock   13   Tsineng

Sonstraal   21   13   Hotazel   Ga-Mopedi   Lykso

Dedeben   R31   61   132

Faans Grove   **KORANNABERG** 1550m   Witloop   R380   Soeding   Moffat's Mission Church 1833   N14

29   Mamathwane   Mothibistat

orthern   Cape   Sutton   50   Kuruman   13

23   20   Vlermuisvlakte   52   Eye of Kuruman

Markramsdraai   26   R372   66

45   15   9   Wincanton   16   R31

12   Dibeng   18   **KURUMAN HILLS**   Bekker

War Graves 1897   Kathu   42   R373   Blikfontein   32

41   35   Sishen   12   58

Moeswal   *Langkloof*   1855m

War Graves 1877   Droespruit   Mookaneng   Wonderwerk Caves

24   Langberg   Lohatlha

Olifantshoek   5   Lohatlha   R31

Vroeggedeel   21   Glosam   31   Danielskuil   Swartputs

160   N14   Vrolik   56   R385   Palingpan   52

Bokkoppie

Blinkklip

22° **To Upington**   23° **To Postmasburg**   24°

5   **6**   **12**   **7**   **8**

Copyright ©Map Studio

Capital or City	Secondary Town	Major Airport	Toll Route	Game & Nature Reserves
Chief Administrative Town	Other Town	Airfield	Toll Plaza	Marsh
Major Town	Settlement	Accommodation	Place of Interest / Historical Site / Border Control / Major Spot Height	Waterfall

Copyright © Map Studio

Freeway & National Road
Principal Trunk Road
Main Road
Secondary Road
Distances in Kilometres
Mountain Passes
Railway
International & Provincial Boun

To Burgersfort   To Ohrigstad   To Satara

KRUGER NATIONAL PARK

SWAZILAND

MBABANE

Manzini

NELSPRUIT

LEBOMBOBERG

MOÇAMBIQ

Matola

Bela Vista

Maputo

Mpumalanga

BALELESBERG

Selected place names and features:

Kennedy's Vale, Glen Cowie, Buffelsvlei, Joubertbrug, Pilgrims Rest, Graskop, Bushbuckridge, Newington, Londolozi, Mala Mala, Tshokwane, Orpen Dam, Macaena, Massintonto

Geological Exposure, Maartenshoop, Krugerpost, Kowyn Pass, Marite, Sabi-Sabi, Jakkalsbessie, Bushveld Camp

Lydenburg, Ohrigstad Dam N.R., Mauchsberg, Kiepersol, Hazyview, Paul Kruger Gate, Skukuza, Lower Sabie, Machatuine

Erts, Roossenekal, De Berg Pass, Sabie, Long Long Pass, Hendriksdal, Numbi Gate, Pretoriuspkop, Jock of the Bushveld, Afsaal

Klipskool, Sudwala Caves, Brondal, Witrivier, Plaston, KaNyamazane, Berg-en-dal, Hectorspruit, Malelane Gate, Crocodile Bridge, Sabie, Chinhanguanine

Laersdrif, Kwena Dam, Karino, Mthethomusha Game Res., Malelane, Komatipoort, Ressano Garcia, Lebombo, Incomati

Dullstroom, Schoemanskloof, Elands River Valley, Kaapsehoop, Kaapmuiden, Kaalrug, Moamba

Machadodorp, Waterval-Boven, Krugerhof, N.Z.A.S.M. Tunnel, Noordkaap, Jeppe's Reef, Avoca, SEE PAGES 44-45, Pessene, Marracue

Belfast, Dalmanutha, Wonderfontein, Mpumalanga, Bothasnek, First Stock Exchange, Hhohho, Matsomo, Ngonini, Manana, Namaacha, Machava, Matola

Carolina, Nelshoogte, Jambila, Barberton, Saddleback, Bulembu, Piggs Peak, Herefords, Sihhoye, Lomahasha, Goba, Maputo

Warburton, Lochiel, Hartbeeskop, Oshoek, Forbes Reef, Malolotja Nat. Res., Bushman Paintings, Croydon, Simunye, Mlawula Nature Reserve, Changalane

Breyten, Chrissiesmeer, Waverley, Lundzi, Swazi Market, Mlilwane N.R., Mhlambanyatsi, Lusutfu, Malkerns, Mpaka, Siteki, Lubhuku, Bela Vista

Ermelo, Holbank, Bankkop, Amsterdam, Nerston, Sandlane, Bhunya, Loyengo, Mankayane, Sidvokodvo, Sipofaneni, Mkhaya N.R., Big Bend

Sheepmoor, Iswepe, Emahlatini, Sicunusa, Kubutsa, Sithobela, Ndumo Game Reserve, Catuane, Tembe Elephant Reserve

Piet Retief, Anysspruit, Mineral Baths, Gege, Bothashoop, Nhlangano, Hlatsikhulu, Maloma, Nsoko, Cecil Macks Pass, Ingwavuma, Lake Sibaya

Wittenberg, Dirkiesdorp, Mahamba, Berbice, Mhlosheni, Hluthi, Onverwacht, Golela, Lavumisa, Pongolapoort Dam

Latemanek, Braunschweig, Commondale, Pongola, Luneberg, Grootspruit, Kingholm, Candover, Jozini, Pongolapoort Nature Reserve, Mbaswan

Wakkerstroom, Groenvlei, Paulpietersburg, Bivane, Itala Nature Reserve, Magudu, Nkoakoni, Ubombo, SEE PAGES 40-41

Madadeni, Utrecht, Mpemvana, Zungwini, Hot Springs, Louwsburg, Mkuze, Mkuzi Game Reserve, Phinda Resource Reserve, The Greater St. Lucia Wet

Ozizweni, Ballengeich, Kingsley, Hlobane, P.L. Uys Memorial, Vryheid, Alpha, Ngome, Thokazi, Bayala

Dannhauser, Bloedrivier, Scheepersnek, Raadsaal and Fort of New Republic, Steilrand, Swart Umfolozi, Nongoma, Leven Poin

Battle of Talana, Battle of Blood River 1838, Prince Imperial 1879 Monument, Calvert, Gluckstadt, Kwaceza, SEE PAGES 40-41, St. Lucia Reserve, Cape Vidal

Glencoe, Dundee, SEE PAGES 42-43, Nondweni, Nqutu, Nhlazatshe, Mahlabatini, Hluhluwe Umfolozi, Huhluwe, Lake St. Lucia, Bushlands

To Ladysmith   To Ulundi   To Mtubatuba

To Witbank, To Hendrina, To Bethal

Legend:

N1 / under construction / untarred	Freeway & National Road
R33	Principal Trunk Road
R523 / under construction / untarred	Main Road
	Secondary Road
15 22	Distances in Kilometres
	Mountain Passes
	Railway
	International & Provincial Boundary

5 10 20 30 40 50km

33° 34° To Quissico 35°

23 Malaira Zandamela
Mazivila 37 67 Madender Lagoa Quissico
Chissano EN1 Chidenguele Lagoa Inhampavala
17 30 31 45 Lagoa Nhanzume
Xinavane 25 13 Chongoene
Macia 9 Praia do
33 Xai-Xai Chongoene
408 Praia do Xai-Xai —25°

A

Praia do Bilene
20 Lagoa Uembje
Manhiça Lagoa Muandje
Lagoa Pati

INDIAN OCEAN

B

Ilha da Inhaca —26°
Cabo de Santa Maria
Santa Maria

Machangulo

Ponta Milibangalala

C

Lagoa Piti

nta do Ouro
onta do Ouro —27°
Bay
Bay
Bay Nature Reserve
er Point

D

oland Marine Reserve

The African Jacana is a bird found in the St. Lucia Wetlands Nature Reserve

E

—28°

34° 35°

☐ Capital or City	◉ Secondary Town
◉ Chief Administrative Town	○ Other Town
○ Major Town	· Settlement

✈ Major Airport
Airfield
Accommodation

• Place of Interest
★ Historical Site
Border Control

Ⓣ Toll Route
Ⓣ Toll Plaza
▲ Major Spot Height

Game & Nature Reserves
Marsh
Waterfall

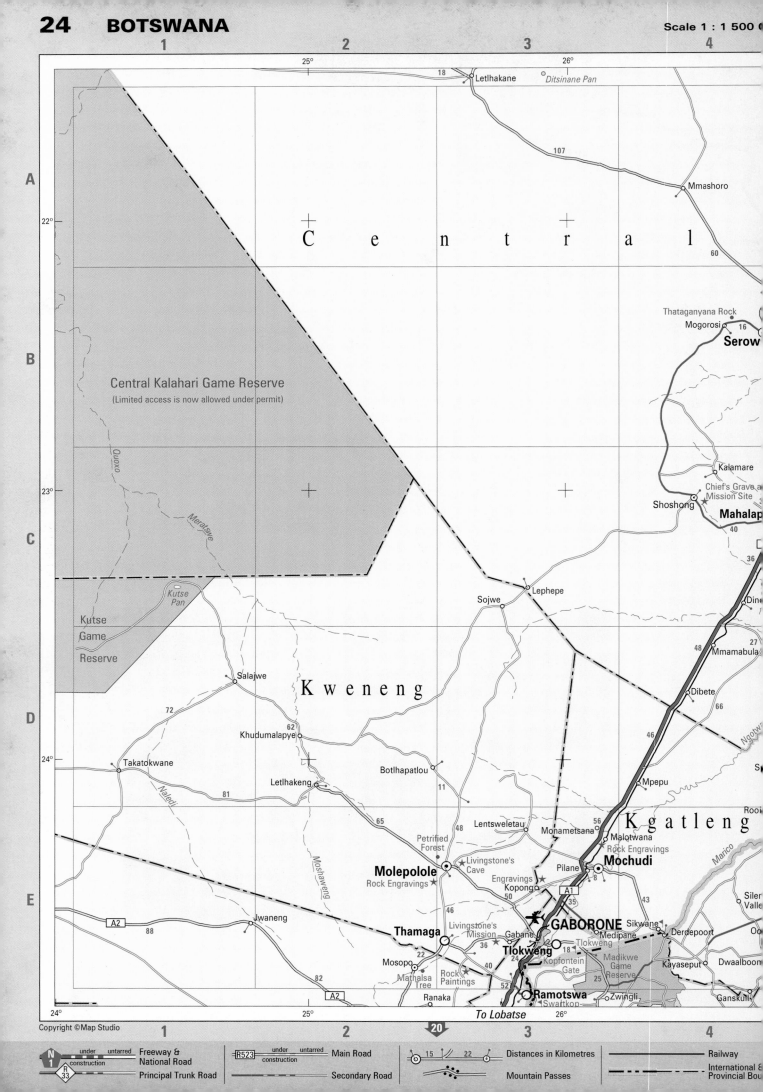

18
Letlhakane   *Ditsinane Pan*

107

A

Mmashoro

22°

C   e   n   t   r   a   l

60

Thataganyana Rock
Mogorosi   16

Serow

B

Central Kalahari Game Reserve
(Limited access is now allowed under permit)

Kalamare

Quoxo

Chief's Grave &
Mission Site

23°

Shoshong   **Mahalap**

Meratswe

40

C

36

Lephepe

Kutse Pan

Sojwe   Din

Kutse
Game
Reserve

48   Mmamabula   27

Salajwe   **K w e n e n g**

Dibete

72

66

62

Khudumalapye

46

D

24°

Takatokwane

Botlhapatlou

81

Letlhakeng

11

Naledi

65

Lentsweletau

56   **K g a t l e n g**

48

Monametsana

Petrified
Forest   *Moshaweng*

Malotwana
Rock Engravings

Rooi

Molepolole   Livingstone's
Rock Engravings   Cave   Engravings   Pilane   **Mochudi**

Kopong   8

43

Sile
Valle

50

A1

E

46

35

Jwaneng

Livingstone's
Mission   **GABORONE**   Sikwane

A2

Thamaga   Gabane   Tlokweng   Medipane   Derdepoort   Oo

88

36   **Tlokweng**   18   Kayaseput   Dwaalboom

Mosopo   22   40   24   Kopfontein   Madikwe   Gate   Game   Reserve

82   Mathalsa   Rock   25   Ganskull
Tree   Paintings   52

A2   Ranaka   **Ramotswa**   Zwingli   Gans
Swaltkop

24°   *To Lobatse*

N	under	untarred	Freeway &	R523	under	untarred	Main Road	15	22	Distances in Kilometres		Railway
1	construction		National Road		construction							International &
R 33			Principal Trunk Road				Secondary Road			Mountain Passes		Provincial Bou

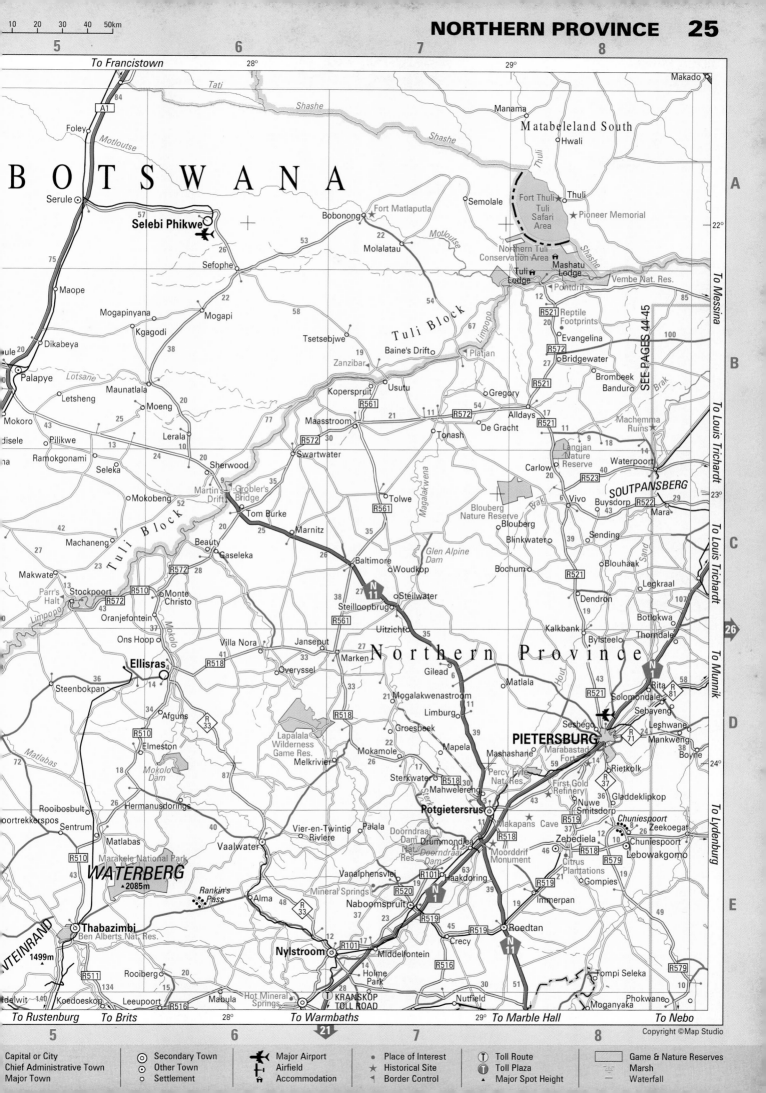

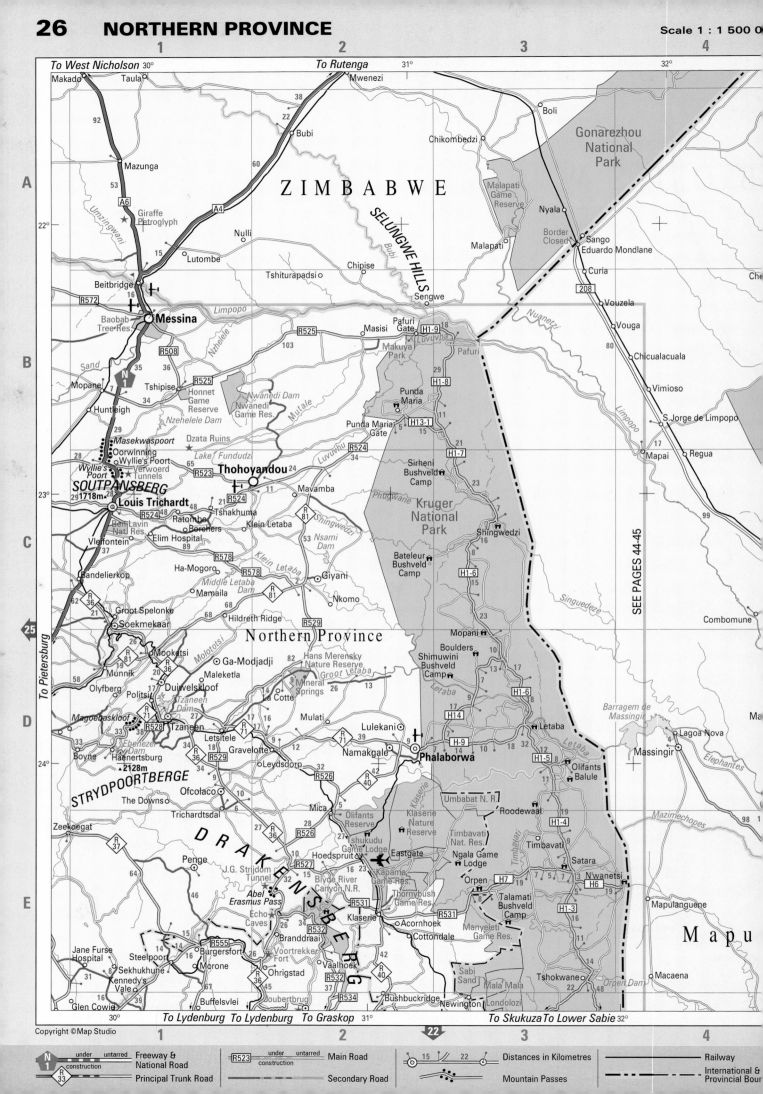

0 5 10 20 30 40 50km

5 **6** **7** **8**

33° 34° *To Save* 35°

Massangena

Parque Nacional de Zinave

Luido

Macovane 252 Inhassoro
15

A

50

Chico

Cometela

Tessolo

Pambarra
EN1

Madade

8 Vilankulo
212

Mabote

22°

21

Rio Zinhazane

Rio Xipembe

32

Uoteche

Chichocane

Lagoa Banamana

Maphinhane

Machaila

Fornos

Cheline

B

66

Mavanza

Parque Nacional de Banhine

Nhachengue

Govuro

26

A lion kill in the Kruger National Park

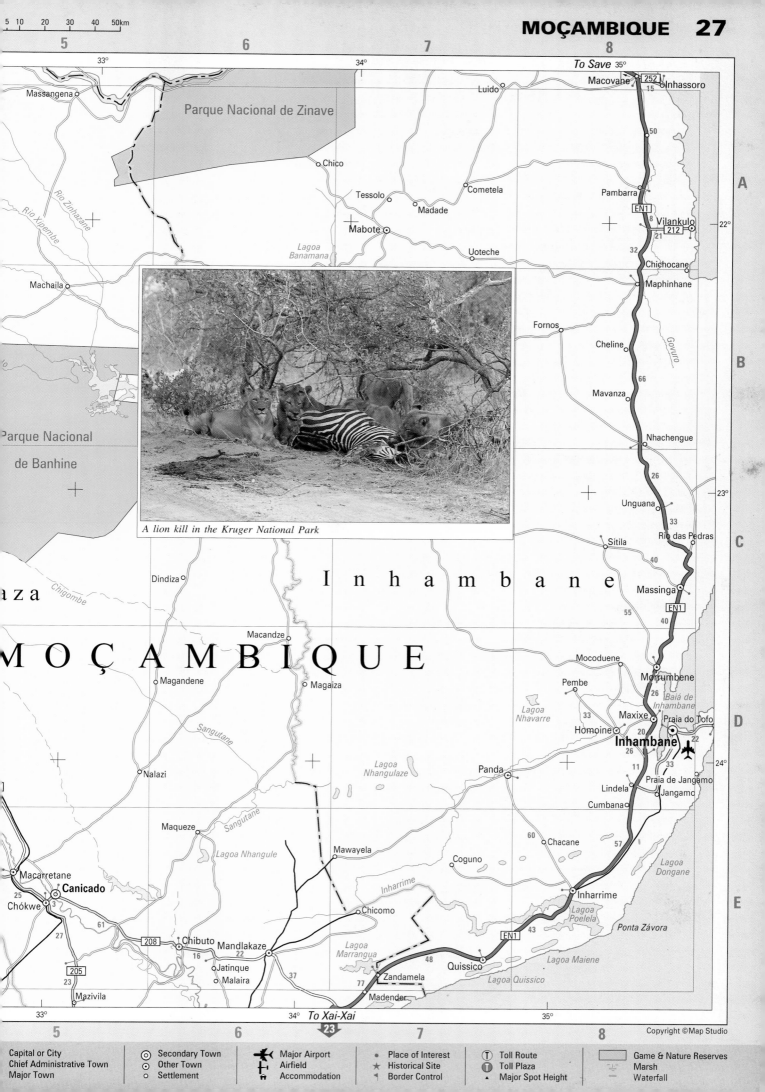

Unguana

23°

33

Sitila

Rio das Pedras

C

za

Chigombe

Dindiza

I n h a m b a n e

Massinga
EN1

40

55

40

MOÇAMBIQUE

Macandze

Mocoduene

Magandene

Magaiza

Pembe

Morrumbene

26 *Baiá de Inhambane*

Lagoa Nhavarre

33

Maxixe

Praia do Tofo

D

Sangutane

Homoine

Inhambane

22

20

26

Nalazi

Lagoa Nhangulaze

Panda

11

33

Praia de Jangamo

24°

Lindela

Jangamo

Cumbana

Maqueze

Sangutane

60

Chacane

57

Lagoa Dongane

Lagoa Nhangule

Mawayela

Coguno

Inharrime

Inharrime

E

Lagoa Poelela

Macarretane

Ponta Závora

Canicado

Chicomo

43

Chókwe
3

25

Lagoa Marrangua

EN1

Lagoa Maiene

27

61

208

22

Chibuto Mandlakaze

48

Quissico

Lagoa Quissico

205

16

Jatinque

77

Zandamela

23

Malaira

37

Madender

Mazivila

33° 34° *To Xai-Xai* 35°

5 **6** 23 **7** **8**

Copyright ©Map Studio

Capital or City — ⊙ Secondary Town — ✈ Major Airport — • Place of Interest — Ⓣ Toll Route — ▭ Game & Nature Reserves
Chief Administrative Town — ⊙ Other Town — Airfield — ★ Historical Site — Ⓣ Toll Plaza — Marsh
Major Town — ○ Settlement — Accommodation — ◄ Border Control — ▲ Major Spot Height — Waterfall

Scale 1 : 12 000 000

0   100   200   300   400

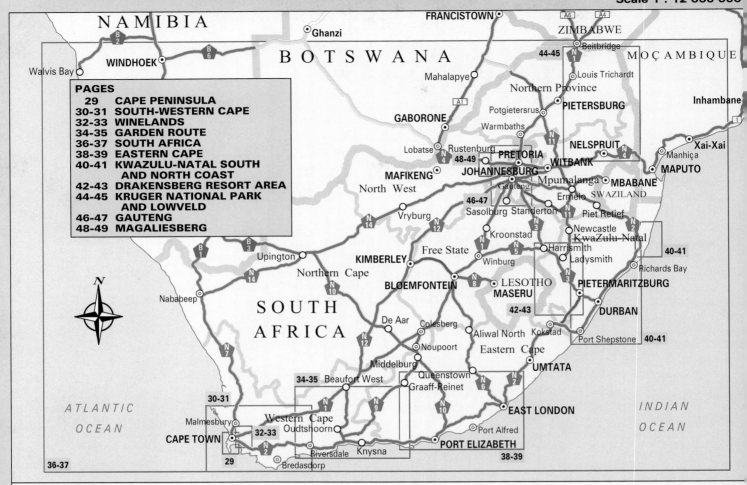

LEGEND TO TOURIST AREA MAPS

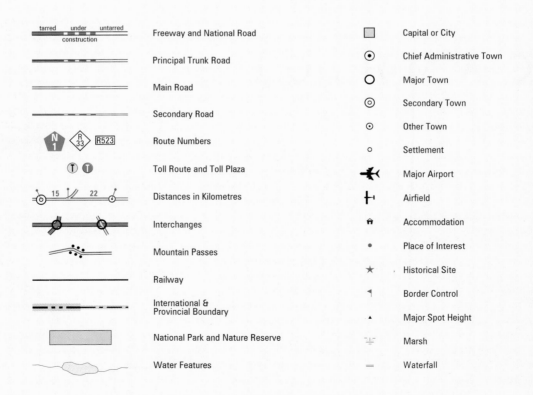

Freeway and National Road	Capital or City
Principal Trunk Road	Chief Administrative Town
Main Road	Major Town
Secondary Road	Secondary Town
Route Numbers	Other Town
Toll Route and Toll Plaza	Settlement
Distances in Kilometres	Major Airport
Interchanges	Airfield
Mountain Passes	Accommodation
Railway	Place of Interest
International & Provincial Boundary	Historical Site
National Park and Nature Reserve	Border Control
Water Features	Major Spot Height
	Marsh
	Waterfall

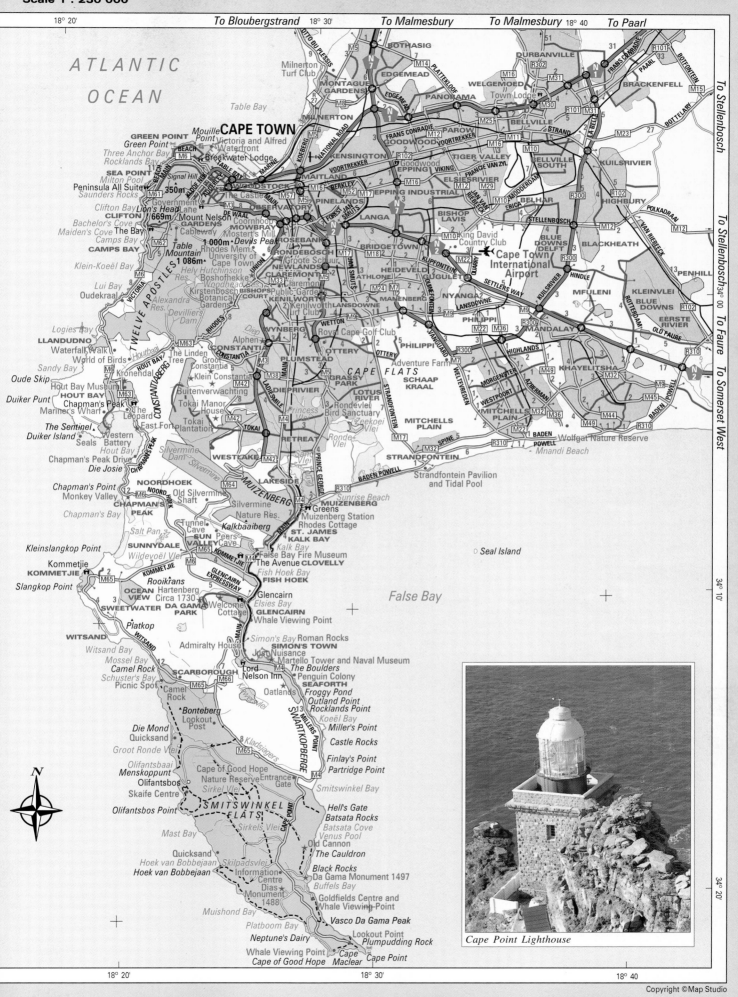

Cape Point Lighthouse

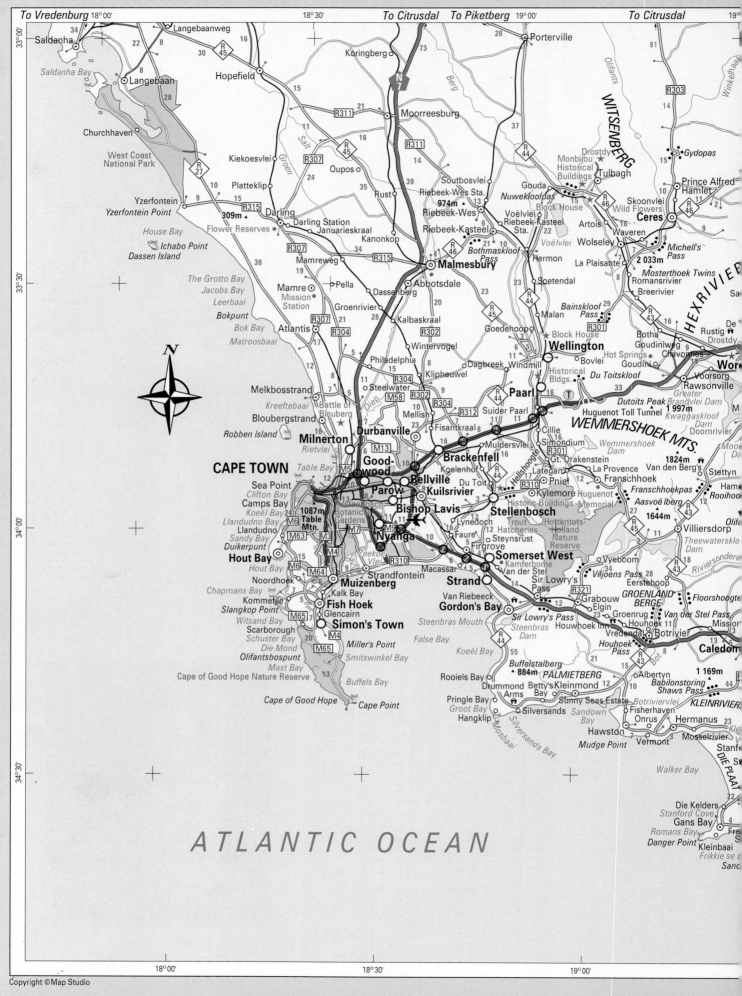

ATLANTIC OCEAN

Copyright © Map Studio

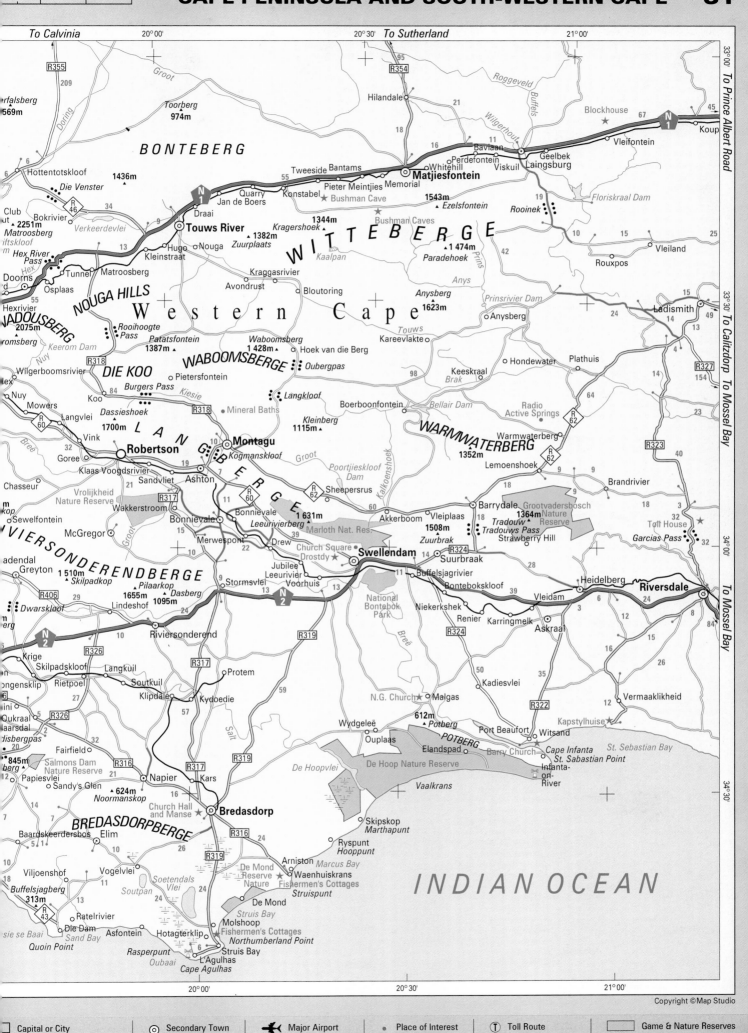

	Capital or City		Secondary Town		Major Airport		Place of Interest	Ⓣ	Toll Route		Game & Nature Reserves
Ⓒ	Chief Administrative Town	◎	Other Town		Airfield	★	Historical Site	Ⓣ	Toll Plaza		Marsh
●	Major Town	○	Settlement		Accommodation	◀	Border Control	▲	Major Spot Height		Waterfall

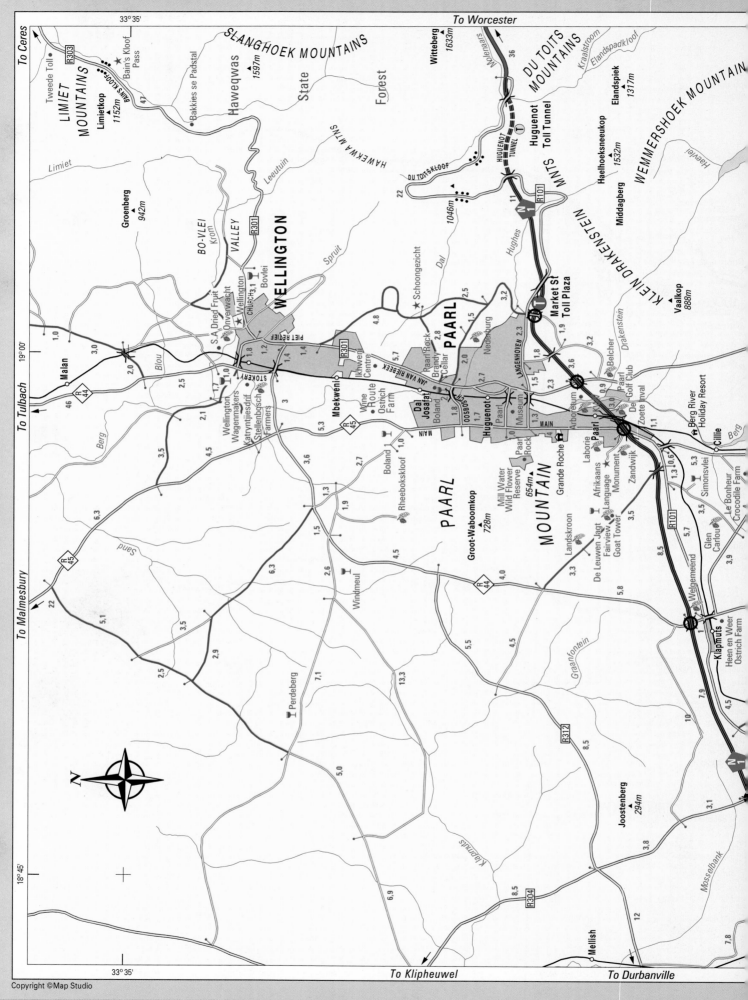

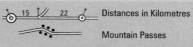

Copyright ©Map Studio

To Klipheuwel — To Durbanville

Legend

N1 / **R33**	Freeway & National Road / Principal Trunk Road
R523	Main Road / Secondary Road
15 / 22	Distances in Kilometres / Mountain Passes
	Railway / International & Provincial Bound

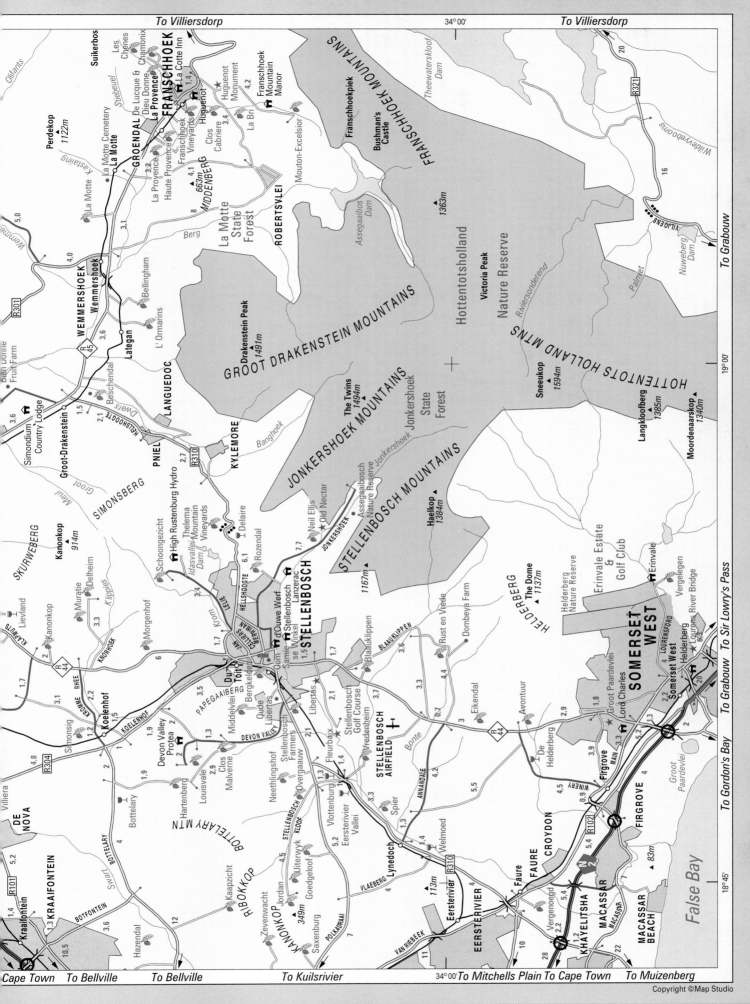

▢ Capital or City	◉ Secondary Town	✈ Major Airport
▢ Chief Administrative Town	◎ Other Town	⊕ Airfield
▢ Major Town	○ Settlement	⌂ Accommodation

• Place of Interest	Ⓣ Toll Route	▭ Game & Nature Reserves
★ Historical Site	Ⓣ Toll Plaza	⚲ Wine Co-ops
◄ Border Control	▲ Major Spot Height	Wineries

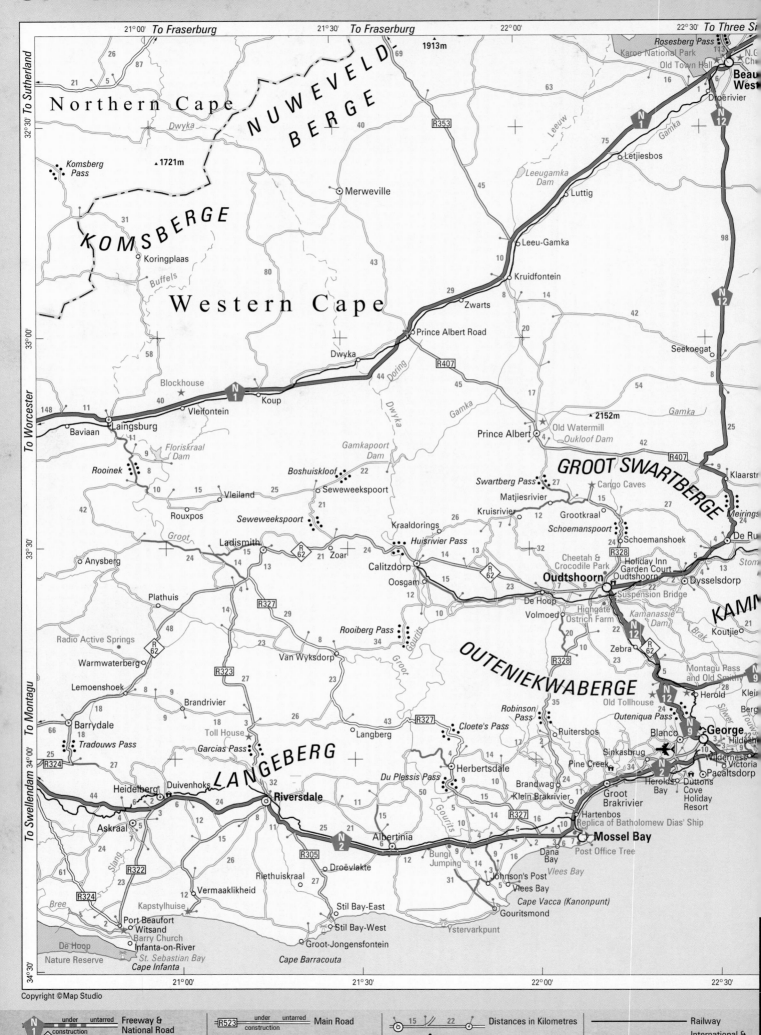

Copyright ©Map Studio

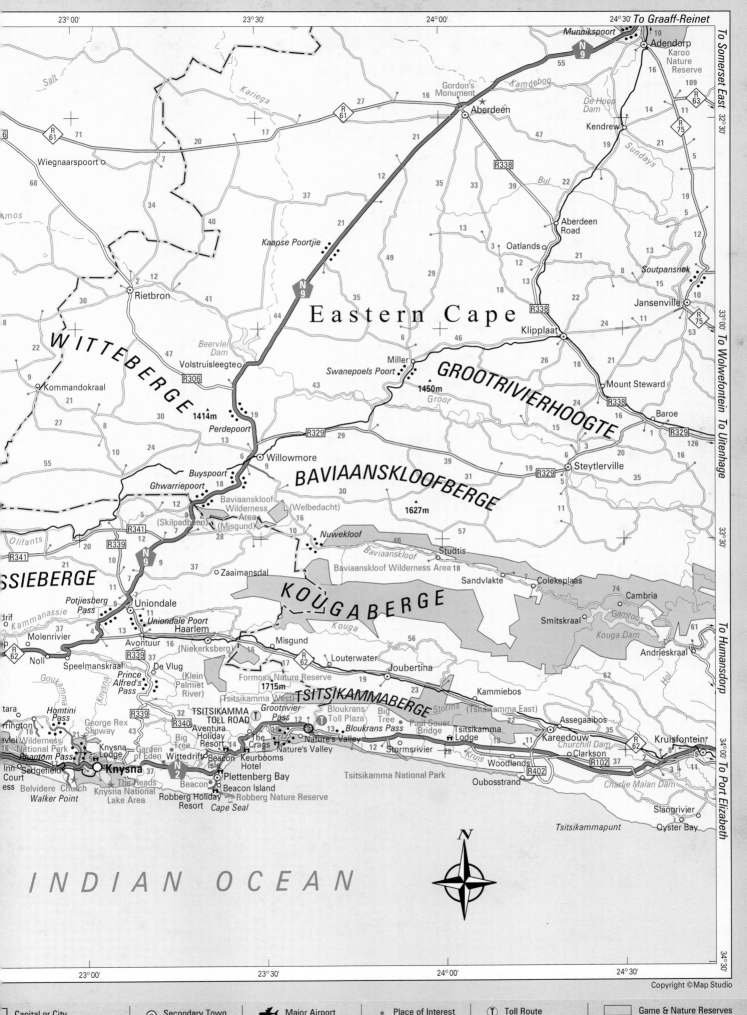

To Somerset East
To Wolwefontein *To Uitenhage*
To Humansdorp
To Port Elizabeth

Eastern Cape

WITTEBERGE

GROOTRIVIERHOOGTE

BAVIAANSKLOOFBERGE

KOUGABERGE

TSITSIKAMMABERGE

INDIAN OCEAN

N

Copyright © Map Studio

Symbol	Description
▢	Capital or City
▢	Chief Administrative Town
○	Major Town
◎	Secondary Town
⊙	Other Town
○	Settlement
✈	Major Airport
✚	Airfield
⌂	Accommodation
●	Place of Interest
★	Historical Site
◄	Border Control
Ⓣ	Toll Route
Ⓣ	Toll Plaza
▲	Major Spot Height
▭	Game & Nature Reserves
	Marsh
	Waterfall

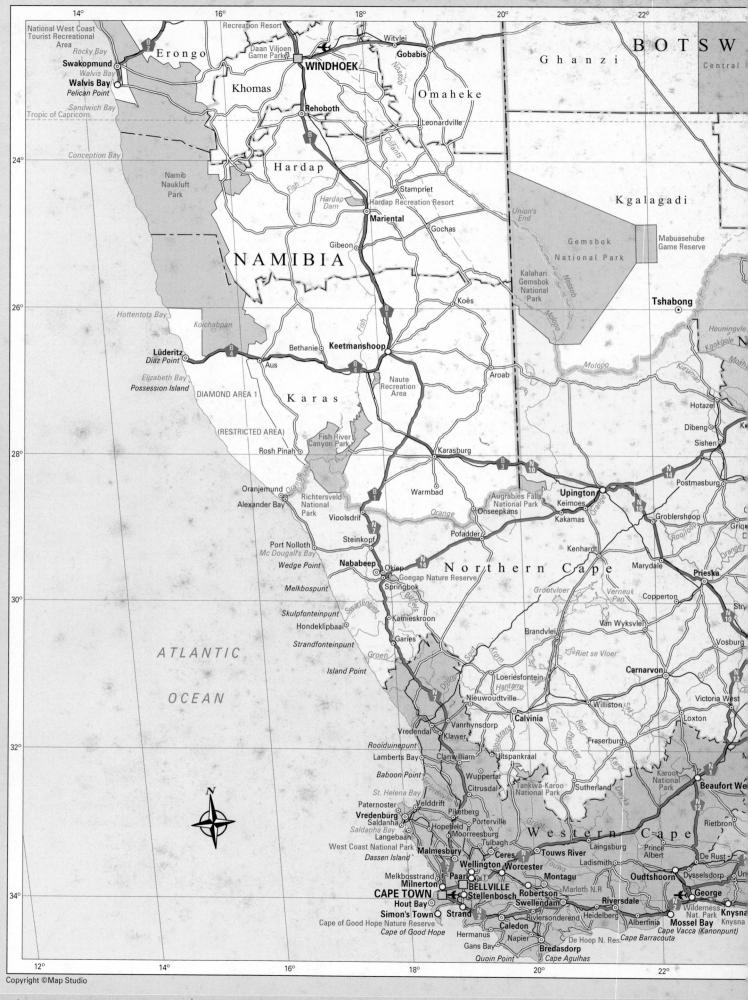

National West Coast Tourist Recreational Area
Rocky Bay
Swakopmund
Walvis Bay
Walvis Bay
Pelican Point
Sandwich Bay
Tropic of Capricorn
Conception Bay

Recreation Resort
Witvlei
Daan Viljoen Game Park
WINDHOEK
Erongo
Khomas
Gobabis

BOTSW
Ghanzi
Central

Rehoboth
Nossob
Omaheke

Leonardville

Olifants

NAMIBIA
Hardap

Stampriet
Hardap Recreation Resort
Hardap Dam
Mariental
Gochas

Gibeon

Kgalagadi
Union's End
Gemsbok National Park
Mabuasehube Game Reserve

Koës
Nossob

Tshabong

Bethanie
Keetmanshoop
Aus

Fish

Naute Recreation Area
Aroab

Kalahari Gemsbok National Park
Molopo

Lüderitz
Diaz Point
Elizabeth Bay
Possession Island
DIAMOND AREA 1

Karasburg

Heuningyle
Kgokgole

Molopo

Hotazel

Dibeng
Sishen

(RESTRICTED AREA)

Karas

Fish River Canyon Park
Rosh Pinah

Warmbad

Augrabies Falls National Park
Keimoes
Upington
Onseepkans
Kakamas

N14

Postmasburg

Kuruman

Mosh

Oranjemund
Orange
Alexander Bay
Richtersveld National Park
Viooolsdrif
Steinkopf
Pofadder
Kenhardt

Orange

Groblershoop

Griq

Port Nolloth
Mc Dougall's Bay
Wedge Point
Nababeep
Okiep
Goegap Nature Reserve
Springbok

Marydale
Prieska

Orange

Northern Cape

Melkbospunt
Kamieskroon

Grootvloer
Verneuk Pan
Copperton

Roolloop

Skulpfonteinpunt
Hondeklipbaai
Garies

Brandvlei
Van Wyksvlei

N10
Stry

Strandfonteinpunt
Island Point

Groen
Sout

Riet se Vloer

Carnarvon

Victoria West

Krom
Loeriesfontein
Hantams

Williston

Loxton

Groen

Vredendal
Vanrhynsdorp
Klawer
Nieuwoudtville

Calvinia

N12

Roolduinepunt
Lamberts Bay
Clanwilliam
Uitspankraal

Fish
Fraserburg

Baboon Point
Wuppertal
Citrusdal

Sutherland

Karoo National Park

N1

St. Helena Bay
Paternoster
Velddrif
Piketberg
Porterville
Tankwa-Karoo National Park
Riet
Laingsburg
Prince Albert

Beaufort We

Vredenburg
Saldanha
Hopefield
Moorreesburg
Tulbagh
Ceres

Rietbron

N12

Langebaan
Saldanha Bay
West Coast National Park
Dassen Island
Malmesbury
Wellington
Worcester
Touws River
Laingsburg
Ladismith
Oudtshoorn
De Rust

Melkbosstrand
Paarl
Montagu
Prince Albert
Dysselsdorp

Western Cape

Milnerton
BELLVILLE
Stellenbosch
Robertson
Marloth N.R
Riversdale
George

CAPE TOWN
Hout Bay
Swellendam
Heidelberg
Albertinia
Mossel Bay
Knysna

Simon's Town
Strand
Caledon
Riviersonderend
Wilderness Nat. Park
Knysna

Cape of Good Hope Nature Reserve
Cape of Good Hope
Hermanus
Napier
Bredasdorp
De Hoop N. Res.
Cape Vacca (Kanonpunt)

Gans Bay
Quoin Point
Bredasdorp
Cape Barracouta

Cape Agulhas

ATLANTIC OCEAN

N

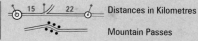

	under construction	untarred	
N1			Freeway & National Road
R33			Principal Trunk Road
R523	under construction	untarred	Main Road
			Secondary Road
15 ⊙——⊙ 22			Distances in Kilometres
			Mountain Passes
			Railway
			International & Provincial Bounda

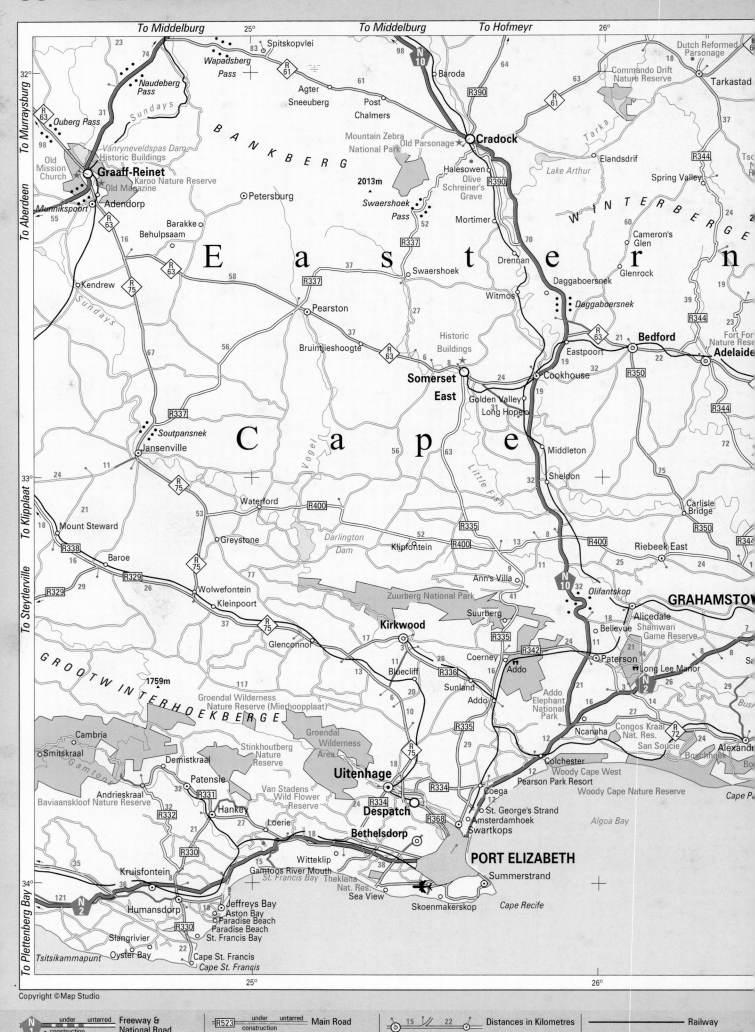

Port Elizabeth beachfront

Copyright © Map Studio

Capital or City	◉ Secondary Town	✈ Major Airport	● Place of Interest	Ⓣ Toll Route	Game & Nature Reserves
Chief Administrative Town	⊙ Other Town	Airfield	★ Historical Site	Ⓣ Toll Plaza	Marsh
Major Town	○ Settlement	Accommodation	▲ Major Spot Height		Waterfall

CONTINUED IN INSET

Hluhluwe Umfolozi Park

K w a Z u l u - N a t a l

Key places: Riverview, Mtubatuba, Kwa Mbonambi, Richards Bay, Empangeni, Felixton, Port Dunford, Port Durnford Lighthouse, Raffia Palms, Mtunzini, Mtunzini Toll Plaza, Hudley, Dokodweni Toll Plaza, Mzingwane, Nyezane, Battle of Tugela 1838, Tugela Mouth, Mandini Toll Plaza, Fort Pearson, Ultimatum Tree, Zinkwazi Beach, Gingindlovu, Amatikulu, Eshowe, Eshowe North, Fort Nongqai, Entumeni, Nkwalini, Melmoth, Ndundulu, Mtonjaneni, Ulundi, Ulundi 1879, Nodwengu, Ilangakazi, Mahlabatini, Ondini, Umunywana, Nhlazatshe, Hlabisa, Hlobane, Babanango, Dingaan's Kraal, Randalhurst, Osborn, Nkandla, Dlolwana, Qudeni, Mangeni, Silutshana, Nqutu, Nondweni, Isandhlwana, Rorke's Drift, Vant's Drift, Elandskraal, Helpmekaar, Pomeroy, Keate's Drift, Muden, Weenen, Greytown, Kranskop, Die Kop 1142 m, The Ranch, Cetshwayo's Grave, Tugela Ferry, Tugela Gorge, Ahrens, Sevenoaks, New Hanover, Dalton, Noodsberg, Wartburg, Harburg, Bruyns Hill, Albert Falls, Howick, Lions River, Stanger, Darnall, Blythdale Beach, Prinley Manor Beach, Sheffield Beach, Salt Rock, Shaka's Rock, Umhlali, Shakaskraal, Glendale, Groutville, Melville, Aldinville, Umvoti Toll Plaza, Shaka's Memorial, Nyoni, Mandini, Sundumbili, Isithebe, Newark, Fort Mtombeni, okwaSizabantu Mission, Mapumulo, Otimati, Mount Elias 938 m, General Louis Botha's Birthplace, Battle of Nsuze 1906, Nsuze, Fawnleas, Tongaat, York, Mersey, Mpolweni, Seven Oaks, Glencoe, Dundee, Battle of Talana, Hattingspruit, Wasbank, Damhauser, Ntabebomvu, Van Rooyen, Battle of Blood River 1838, Prince Imperial 1879 Monument, Bloedrivier, Ulolwe.

Reserves/areas: Hluhluwe Game Reserve, Umfolozi Game Reserve, Lake Eteza Nature Reserve, Enseleni Nature Reserve, Richards Bay Game Reserve, Umlalazi Nature Reserve, Coward's Bush Monument, Bulawayo Site of Shaka's Kraal, Fort Kwa-Mondi, Karkloof N.R., Craigie Burn N.R., Albert Falls N.R., Valley of 1000 Hills, Otto's Bluff.

To Mkuze, To Nongoma, To Vryheid, To N11, To Colenso, To Mooi River, To Nottingham Road.

NORTH COAST TOLL ROAD • NORTH COAST TOLL ROUTE

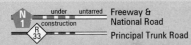
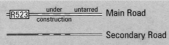
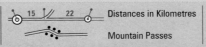
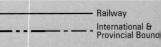

Legend: Freeway & National Road — under construction / untarred; Principal Trunk Road; Main Road — under construction / untarred; Secondary Road; Distances in Kilometres; Mountain Passes; Railway; International & Provincial Boundary.

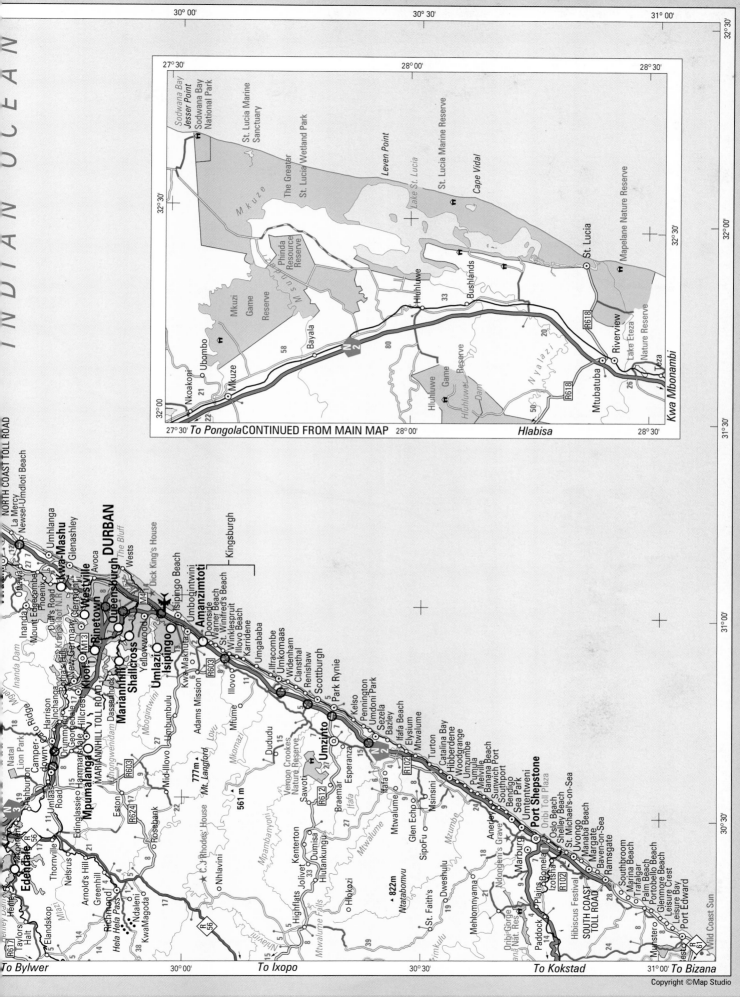

INDIAN OCEAN

Inset map (Continued from main map)

27° 30' 28° 00' 28° 30'

Sodwana Bay
Jesser Point
Sodwana Bay National Park
St. Lucia Marine Sanctuary
The Greater St. Lucia Wetland Park
St. Lucia Marine Reserve
Leven Point
Lake St. Lucia
Cape Vidal
St. Lucia
Mapelane Nature Reserve
Mkuze
Phinda Resource Reserve
Mkuzi Game Reserve
Bushlands
Hluhluwe
Riverview
Lake Eteza Nature Reserve
Teza
Mtubatuba
Kwa Mbonambi
Mkuze
Nkoakoni
Ubombo
Bayala
Hluhluwe Game Reserve
Hluhluwe Dam
Nyalazi
Hlabisa

To Pongola CONTINUED FROM MAIN MAP

R618

N2

Main map

NORTH COAST TOLL ROAD

DURBAN
La Mercy
Newsel-Umdloti Beach
Umhlanga
Glenashley
Kwa Mashu
Avoca
Inanda
Mount Edgecombe
Phoenix
The Bluff
Dick King's House
Westville
Germany
Wests
Kingsburgh
Queensburgh
Pinetown
Hillcrest
Mariannhill
Shallcross
Yellowwood
Umlazi
Isipingo
Isipingo Beach
Umbogintwini
Amanzimtoti
Warner Beach
St. Winifred's Beach
Kwa-Makhutha
Doonside
Illovo Beach
Karridene
Umgababa
Adams Mission
Illovo
Umkomaas
Widenham
Clansthal
Renishaw
Scottburgh
Park Rynie
Kelso
Pennington
Sezela
Umdoni Park
Ifafa Beach
Elysium
Mtwalume
Bazley
Bazley Beach
Ilfracombe

Edendale
Taylors Halt
Richmond
Hela Hela Pass
KwaMagoda
Ndaleni
Thornville
Arnold's Hill
Greenhill
Nelsrus
Nhlavini
C.J.Rhodes' House
777m Mt. Langford
561 m
Dududu
Venon Crookes Nature Reserve
Sawot
Mid-Illovo
Eston
Rosebank
Highflats
Jolivet
Kenterton
Dumisa
Hutankungu
Hlokozi
822m Ntatabomvu
Braemar
Ifafa
Esperanza
Umzinto
Umzumbe
Sipofu
Dweshulu
St. Faith's
Mehlomnyama
Ndongeni's Grave
Hibberdene
Catalina Bay
Woodgrange
Umzumbe
Melville
Banana Beach
Sunwich Port
Southport
Sea Park
Umtentweni
Port Shepstone
Oribi Gorge Nat. Res.
Marburg
Bomela
Izotsha
Oslo Beach
Shelley Beach
St. Michael's-on-Sea
Uvongo
Margate
Manaba Beach
Ramsgate
Southbroom
Marina Beach
Trafalgar
Palm Beach
Portobello Beach
Glenmore Beach
Leisure Bay
Leisure Crest
Port Edward
Wild Coast Sun
Hibiscus Festival
SOUTH COAST TOLL ROAD
Munster
Paddock
Plains
R102
R61

To Bylwer   To Ixopo   To Kokstad   To Bizana

Copyright ©Map Studio

Legend

Symbol	Description
◻	Capital or City
◻	Chief Administrative Town
◻	Major Town
⊙	Secondary Town
⊙	Other Town
○	Settlement
✈	Major Airport
✈	Airfield
⌂	Accommodation
●	Place of Interest
★	Historical Site
◄	Border Control
Ⓣ	Toll Route
Ⓣ	Toll Plaza
▲	Major Spot Height
◻	Game & Nature Reserves
	Marsh
	Waterfall

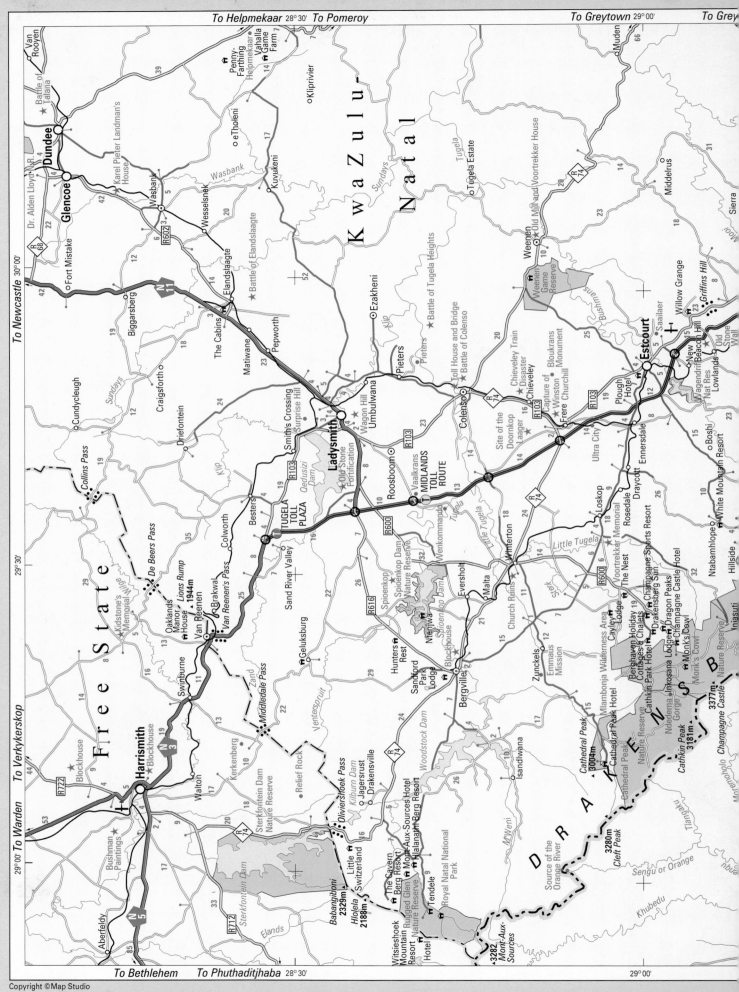

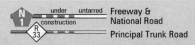
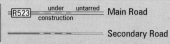

Freeway & National Road

Principal Trunk Road

R523 under construction untarred — Main Road

Secondary Road

15 / 22 Distances in Kilometres

Mountain Passes

Railway

International & Provincial Bour

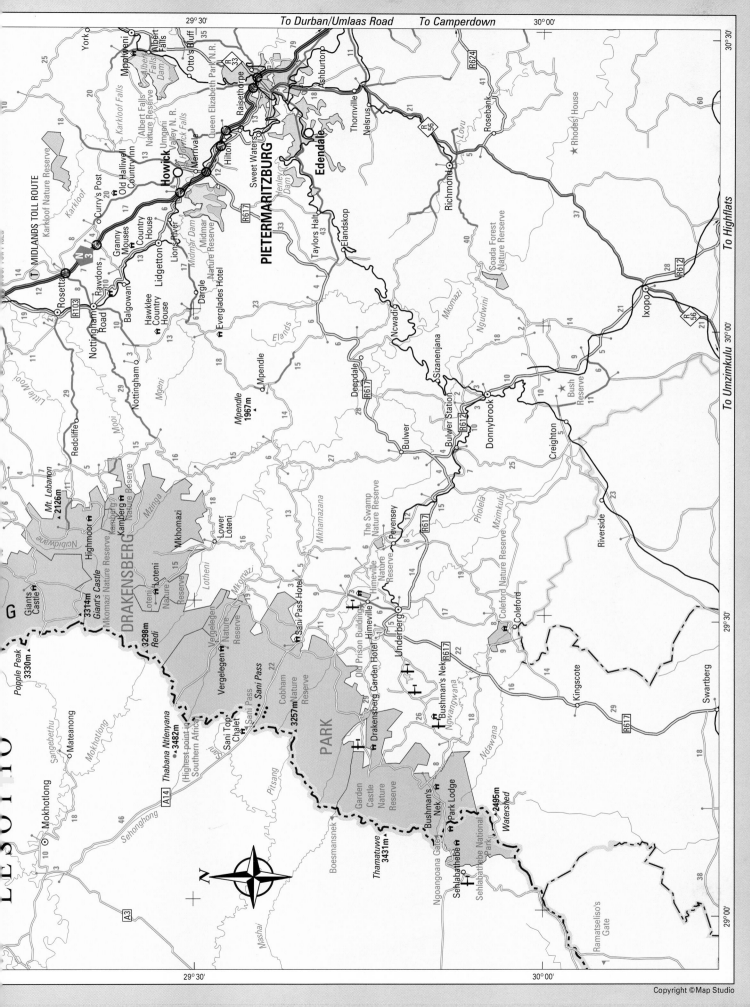

▢ Capital or City	◉ Secondary Town	✈ Major Airport
▢ Chief Administrative Town	◎ Other Town	✈ Airfield
▢ Major Town	○ Settlement	♠ Accommodation

● Place of Interest	Ⓣ Toll Route	▢ Game & Nature Reserves
★ Historical Site	Ⓣ Toll Plaza	Marsh
◀ Border Control	▲ Major Spot Height	Waterfall

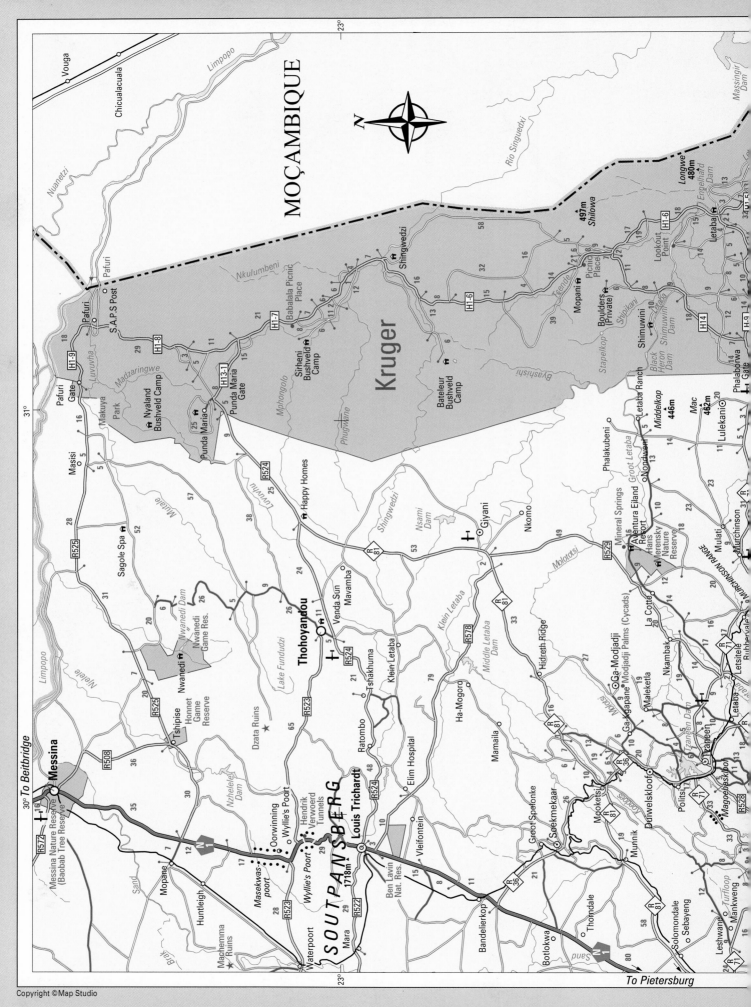

MOÇAMBIQUE

N

Limpopo

Rio Singuedzi

Massingir

Nuanetzi

Vouga

Chicualacuala

Pafuri

S.A.P.S Post

Pafuri

Pafuri Gate

Nkulumbeni

Shingwedzi

Shilowa 497m

Longwe 480m

Engelhard Dam

Lookout Point H1-6

Letaba

Tsende

Mopani

Picnic Place

Boulders (Private)

Shimuwini

Shimuwini Dam

Black Heron Dam

Letaba Ranch

Phalaborwa

Kruger

Babalala Picnic Place

Sirheni Bushveld Camp

H1-7

H1-8

H1-9

Mphongolo

Phugwane

Bateleur Bushveld Camp

Byashishi

Stapelkop

Luvuvha

Madzaringwe

Nyaland Bushveld Camp

Punda Maria

Punda Maria Gate

H13-1

Makuya Park

Masisi

Phalakubeni

Middelkop 446m

Mac 462m

Lulekani

Mineral Springs

Nondweni

Groot Letaba

R524

Happy Homes

Giyani

Nkomo

Nsami Dam

Shingwedzi

Klein Letaba

Aventura Eiland Resort

Werensky Nature Reserve

R529

Luvuvhu

Sagole Spa

R525

Nzhelele

Nwanedi Dam

Nwanedi Game Res.

Lake Fundudzi

Thohoyandou

Venda Sun

Mavamba

Tshakhuma

Klein Letaba

R524

R578

Middle Letaba Dam

Hlidreth Ridge

Ha-Mogoro

R81

Molotatsi

Ga-Kgapane

'Modjadji Palms (Cycads)

Ga-Modjadji

Maleketla

La Cotte

Mulati

Murchinson

MURCHINSON RANGE

Nkambak

Honnet Game Reserve

Tshipise

R525

Dzata Ruins

R523

Ratombo

Elim Hospital

Mamaila

Mödsi

Letsitele

Rubbervale

Duiwelskloof

Tzaneen Dam

Tzaneen

R81

R36

Messina Nature Reserve (Baobab Tree Reserve)

To Beitbridge

Messina

R572

R508

Oorwinning

Wyllie's Poort

Hendrik Verwoerd Tunnels

Louis Trichardt

SOUTPANSBERG 1718m

Ben Lavin Nat. Res.

Vleifontein

R524

Groot Spelonke

Soekmekaar

Mooketsi

R81

Munnik

Politsi

Magoebaskloof

R528

Mopane

Huntleigh

Masekwas-poort

R523

Wyllie's Poort

Mara

R522

Waterpoort

Machemma Ruins

Sand

Bandelierkop

R36

Thorndale

Botlokwa

Solomondale

Sebaveng

Leshwana

Mankweng

R81

Turfloop

Sand

To Pietersburg

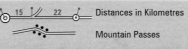

	under construction	untarred	
N1			Freeway & National Road
R33			Principal Trunk Road
R523	under construction	untarred	Main Road
			Secondary Road
15 / 22			Distances in Kilometres
			Mountain Passes
			Railway
			International & Provincial Bound...

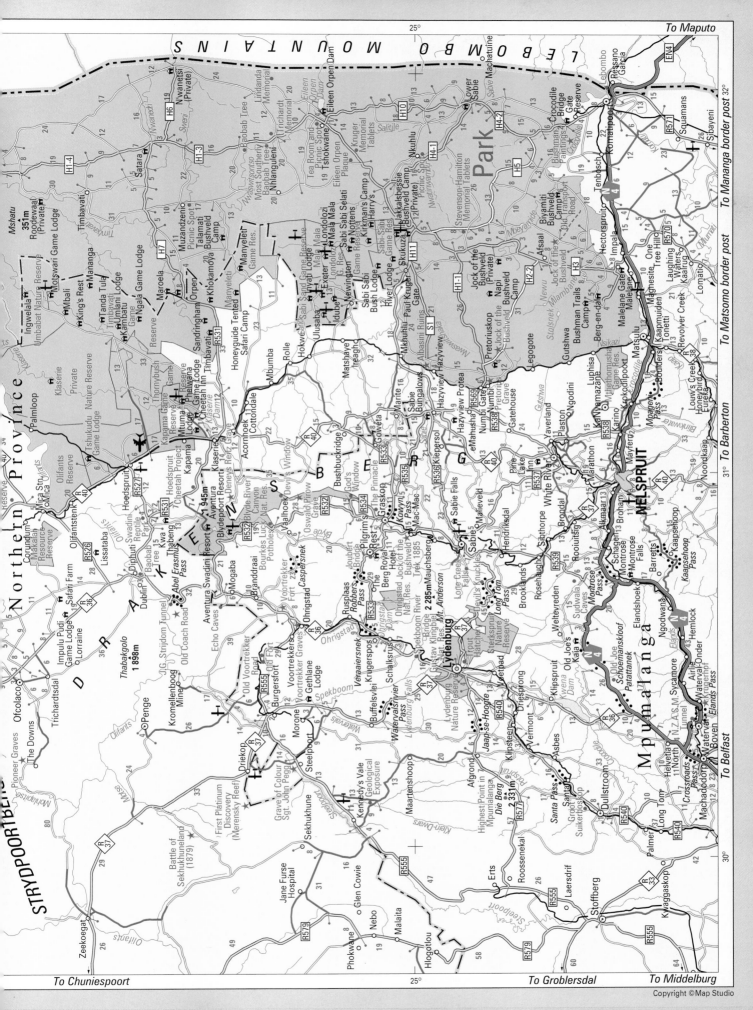

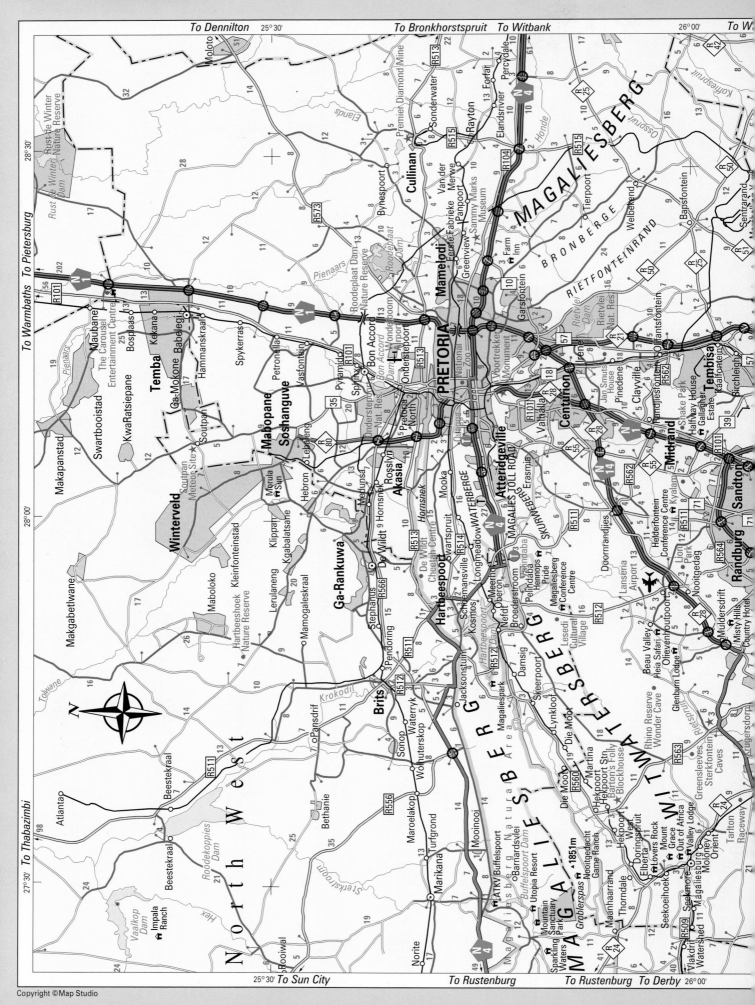

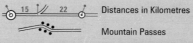

2.5 5 10 15 20km

To Devon To Bethal To Devon 26°30' To Greylingstad

Mpumalanga

Gauteng

To Villiers · To Heilbron 28°00' · To Koppies · To Kroonstad

To Ventersdorp To Carletonville To Potchefstroom 26°30' To Potchefstroom To Potchefstroom To Vredefort

Major towns and places:
JOHANNESBURG, ROODEPOORT, SOWETO, Lenasia, Bekkersdal, Randfontein, Westonaria, Carletonville, BENONI, Boksburg, Brakpan, Germiston, Edenvale, Bedfordview, Alberton, Springs, Kwa-Thema, Tsakane, Duduza, Nigel, Heidelberg, Vosloorus, Katlehong, Tokoza, Balfour, Randvaal, Meyerton, Henley-on-Klip, Daleside, VEREENIGING, Vanderbijlpark, Sasolburg, Sharpeville, Sebokeng, Evaton, Emerdale, Grasmere, Deneysville, Parys, Fochville

SUIKERBOSRAND
Suikerbosrand Nature Reserve
Aventura Heidelbergkloof
Perdekop 1 903m
Aventura Kareekloof
Transport Museum

Midvaal Motor Race Track
Aloe Fjord Resort
Riviera Hotel
Vaal Race Course
Danie Theron Monument
Losberg 1 728m
Vaal Barrage

KROONVAAL TOLL ROUTE

Vaal Dam
Loch Vaal
Vaal

Route numbers: R42, R550, R551, R553, R554, R555, R557, R558, R559, R103, R548, R549, R500, R501, R716, R723, N1, N3, N12, N17, R23, R24, R28, R41, R51, R54, R57, R59, R82

Legend

☐ Capital or City	◉ Secondary Town
◉ Chief Administrative Town	⊙ Other Town
☐ Major Town	○ Settlement

✈ Major Airport	● Place of Interest
Airfield	★ Historical Site
Accommodation	◀ Border Control

Ⓣ Toll Route	☐ Game & Nature Reserves
Ⓣ Toll Plaza	Marsh
▲ Major Spot Height	Waterfall

Copyright © Map Studio

Scale 1 : 300 00

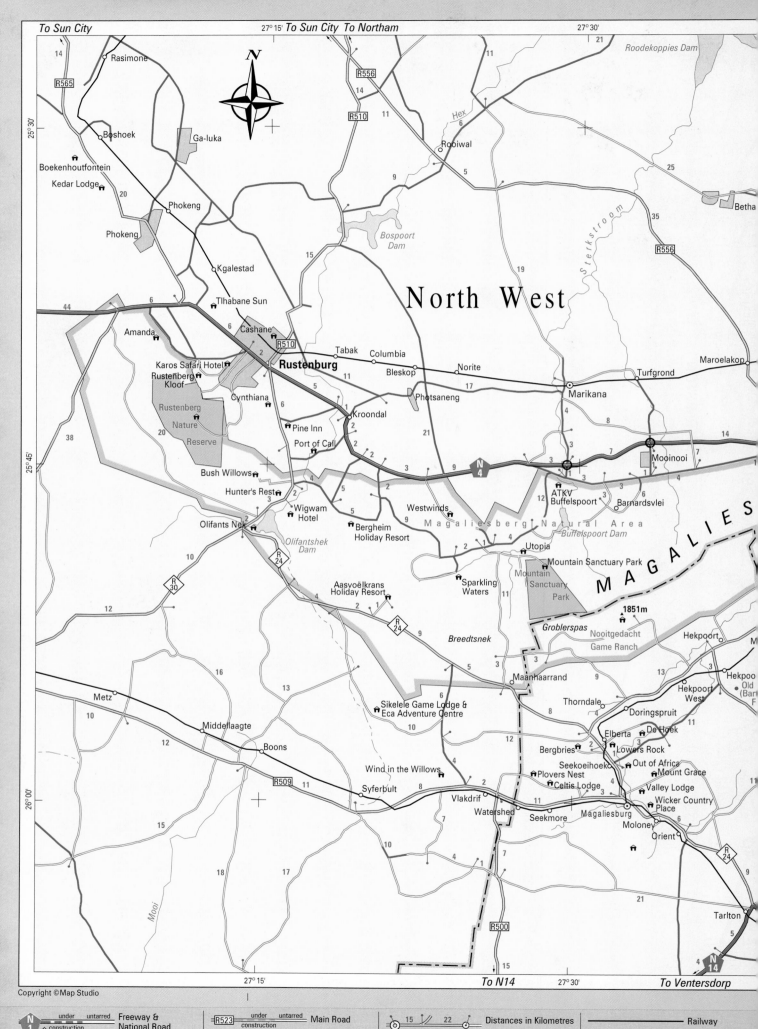

To Sun City
To Sun City To Northam
To N14
27° 30'
To Ventersdorp

Roodekoppies Dam
North West
MAGALIES
MAGALIES

Copyright ©Map Studio

Copyright ©Map Studio

▢ Capital or City	◉ Secondary Town	✈ Major Airport	• Place of Interest	ⓣ Toll Route
▢ Chief Administrative Town	◎ Other Town	✈ Airfield	★ Historical Site	Ⓣ Toll Plaza
○ Major Town	○ Settlement	⌂ Accommodation	◄ Border Control	▲ Major Spot Height

Game & Nature Reserves
Marsh
Waterfall

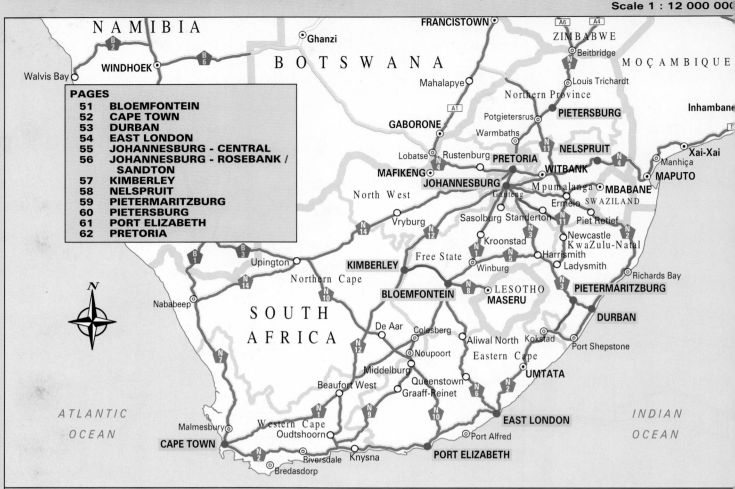

PAGES

LEGEND TO STREET MAPS

Freeway	Major Airport
National Route	Airfield
Main Through Route	Heliport
Other Road	Tourist Information Centre
Route Numbers	Hotel
One-way Street Start / End	Place of Interest
Bridge	National Monument
Railway	Theatre
Station	Cinema
Other Rail	Major Shopping Centre
Built-up Area	Parking
Park	Caravan Park

Lighthouse
Police Station
Community Service
Post Office
Recreation Centre
Library
School
Hospital (24 hour Casualty)
Hospital
Clinic
Spotheight

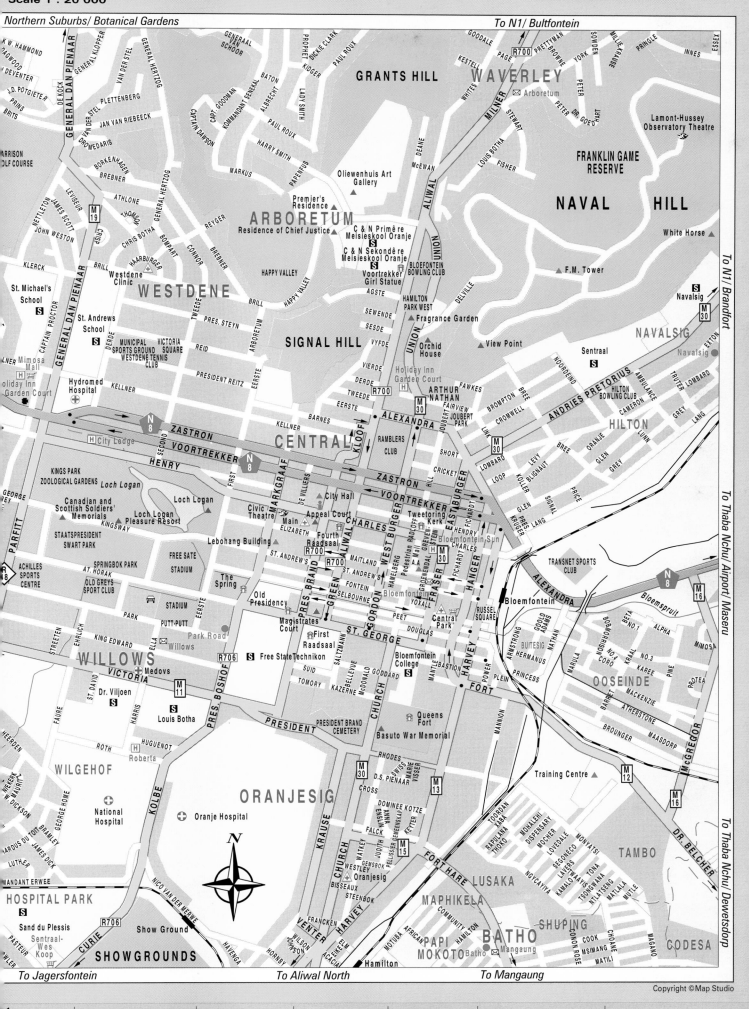

Scale 1 : 20 000

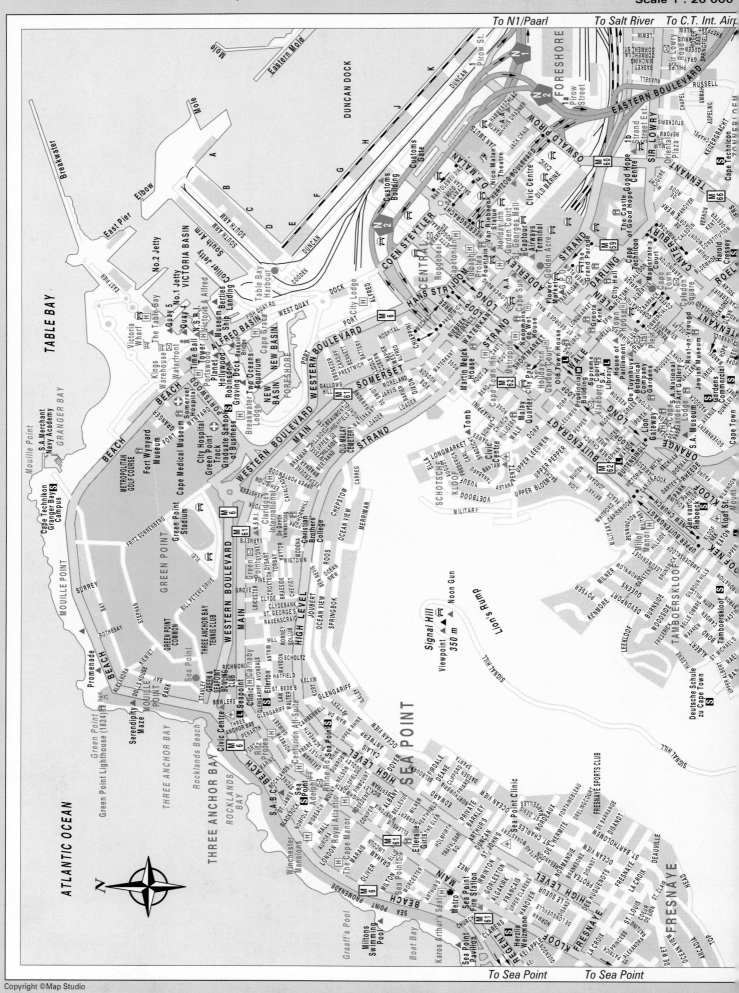

Scale 1 : 20 000
200 400 600m

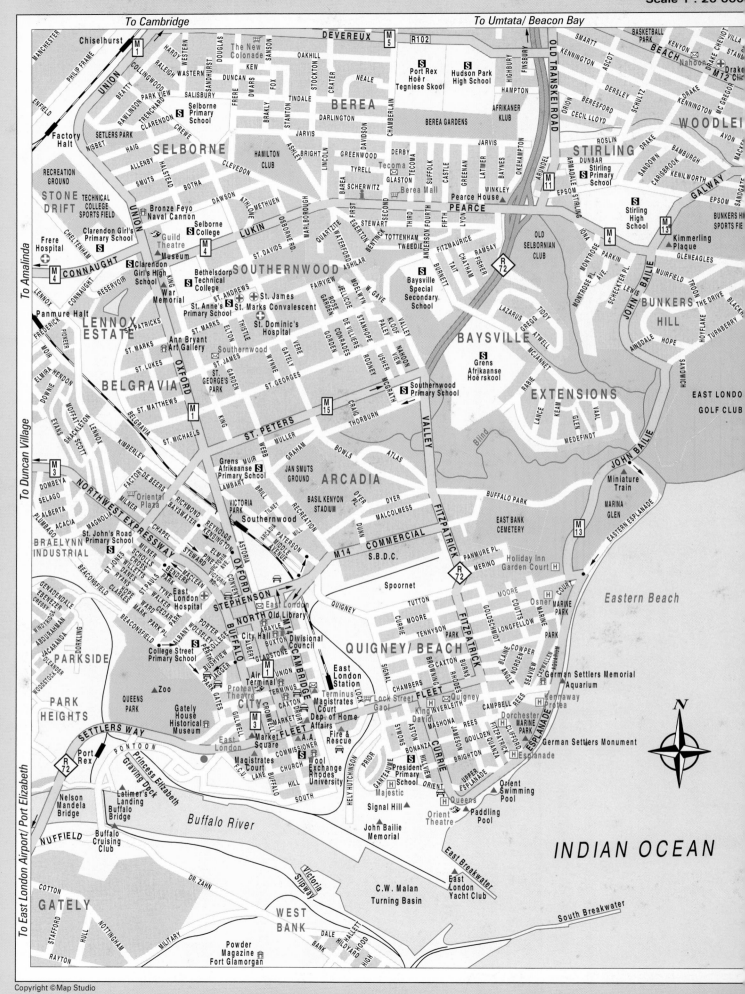

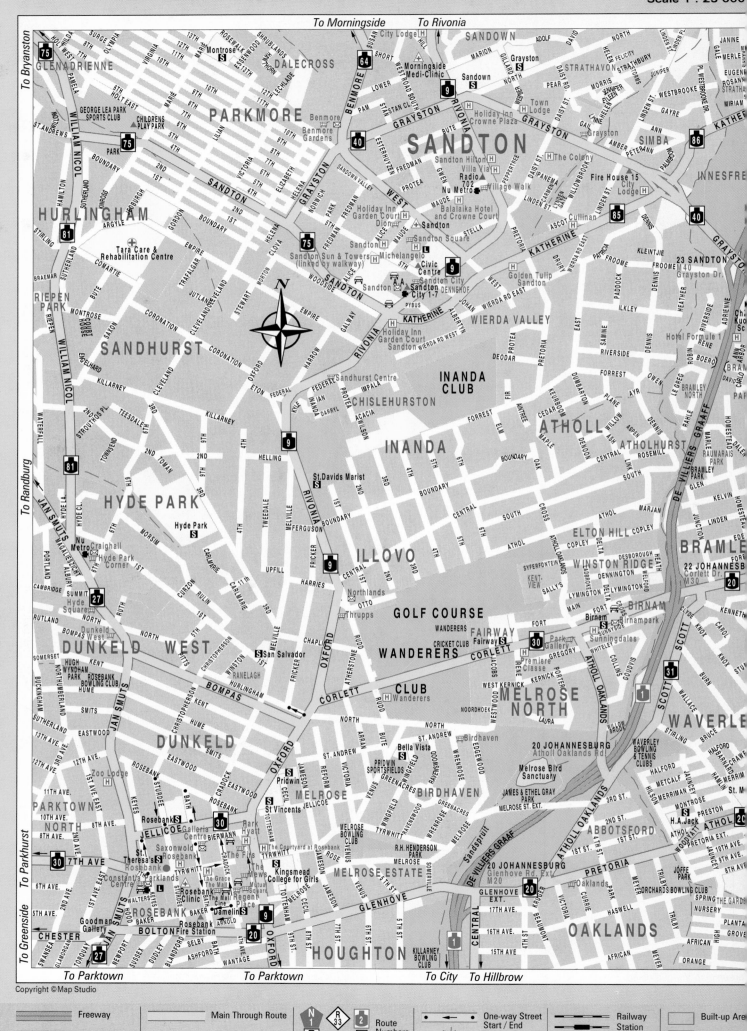

Scale 1 : 20 000

200 400 600m

Symbol	Description		Symbol	Description
	Major Airport			National Monument
	Airfield			Theatre
	Heliport			Cinema
	Tourist Information Centre			Police Station
	Hotel			Community Service
	Place of Interest			Post Office
				Recreation Centre
				Library
				School
				Hospital (24 hour Casualty)
				Hospital
				Clinic
				Parking
				Caravan Park
				Major Shopping Centre

Scale 1 : 20 000

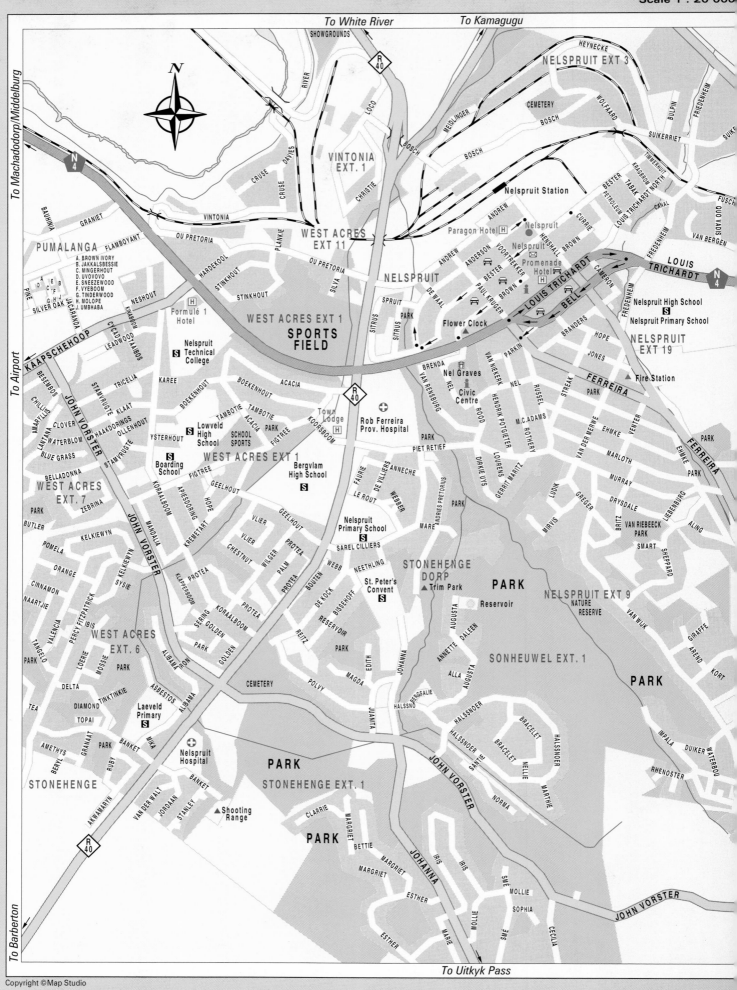

To White River

To Kamagugu

SHOWGROUNDS

NELSPRUIT EXT 3

HEYNECKE

VINTONIA EXT. 1

CEMETERY

WOLFAARD

BOSCH

LOCO

MEIDLINGER

BOSCH

RIVER

BULPIN

FRIEDENHEIM

SUIKERRIET

SUIKE

R40

TIMMERHUIT

KRAGBROM

BESTER TABAK

Nelspruit Station

PETROLEIM NORTH

LOUIS TRICHARDT NORTH

CANAL

FUSCH

QUO VADIS

VAN BERGEN

DAVIES

CRUSE

CHRISTIE

WEST ACRES EXT 11

ANDREW

Paragon Hotel H

Nelspruit H

HENSHALL BROWN

CURRIE

FREDENHEIM

LOUIS TRICHARDT

N4

PUMALANGA

FLAMBOYANT

VINTONIA

OU PRETORIA

A. BROWN IVORY
B. JAKKALSBESSIE
C. MINGERHOUT
D. UVOVOVO
E. SNEEZEWOOD
F. VYEBOOM
G. TINDERWOOD
H. MOLOPE
J. UMBHABA

GRANIET

BAUHINIA

PINE

SILVER OAK

JACARANDA

NESHOUT

HARDEKOOL

STINKHOUT

STINKHOUT

OU PRETORIA

SILVA

NELSPRUIT

ANDREW

ANDERSON

BESTER

VOORTREKKER

Promenade Hotel

Nelspruit High School

Nelspruit Primary School

NELSPRUIT EXT 19

To Machadadorp/Middelburg

N4

Formulé 1 Hotel H

WEST ACRES EXT 1

SPORTS FIELD

SPRUIT

SITRUS

PARK

DE WAAL

PAUL KRUGER

BROWN

Flower Clock

BELL

BRANDERS

HOPE

JONES

FERREIRA PARK

KINABOON

KAAPSCHEHOOP

CYCADHOUT

LEADWOOD

TAAIBOS

Nelspruit Technical College

KAREE

BOEKENHOUT

ACACIA

R40

Town Lodge H

Rob Ferreira Prov. Hospital

BRENDA

VAN NIEKERK

Nel Graves

Civic Centre

NEL

HENDRIK POTGIETER

ROOD

RUSSEL

M.C.ADAMS

ROTHERY

STREAK

Fire Station

FERREIRA

PARK

To Airport

JOHN VORSTER

BESEMBOS

CHILLIES

STAMVRUGTE

KLAAT

HAAKDORINGS

OLLENHOUT

TRICELIA

CLOVER

WATERBLOM

BLUE GRASS

BOEKENHOUT

TAMBOTIE

TAMBOTIE

ACACIA

PARK

FIGTREE

YSTERHOUT

KOORSBOOM

Lowveld High School S

SCHOOL SPORTS

WEST ACRES EXT 1

PARK

PIET RETIEF

VAN RENSBURG

NEL

PARK

DIRKIE UYS

LOURENS

GERRIT MARITZ

VAN DER MERWE

VENTER

EHMKE

MARLOTH

MURRAY

DRYSDALE

GREGER

FERREIRA

PARK

EHNKE

BELLADONNA

WEST ACRES EXT. 7

ZEBRINA

Boarding School

FIGTREE

GEELHOUT

Bergvlam High School S

FAURIE

DE VILLIERS

ANNECHE

WEBBER

MARE

ANDRES PRETORIUS

PARK

LUDIK

MIRVIS

BRITZ

VAN RIEBEECK PARK

LIEBENBURG

ALING

PARK

BUTLER

POMELA

ORANGE

CINNAMON

NAARTJIE

PARK

ZEBRINA

APIESDORING

KREMETART

HOPE

VLIER

VLIER

CHESTNUT

WILGER

PROTEA

PALM

PROTEA

Nelspruit Primary School S

SAREL CILLIERS

NEETHLING

St. Peter's Convent S

STONEHENGE DORP

Trim Park

PARK

Reservoir

NELSPRUIT EXT 9

NATURE RESERVE

SMART

SHEPPARD

VAN WIJK

GIRAFFE

AREND

KORT

VALENCIA

PERCY FITZPATRICK

IBIS

SYSIE

WEST ACRES EXT. 6

MANDALA

KORAALBOOM

SERING

GOLDEN

PARK

GOLDEN

PROTEA

REITZ

BOUEN

DE KOCK

BISSEHOF

RESERVOIR

PARK

WEBB

EDITH

MAGDA

JOHANNA

AUGUSTA

DALEEN

ANNETTE

ALLA

AUGUSTA

PARK

SONHEUWEL EXT. 1

PARK

IMPALA

DUIKER

WATERBOU

RHENOSTER

LOERIE

MOSSIE

PARK

DELTA

DIAMOND

TINKTINKIE

TOPAI

Laeveld Primary S

ASBESTOS

ALIBAMA

MIKA

KLAPPERBOOM

ALIBAMA

CEMETERY

POLVY

JUANITA

BERGSALIE

HALSSNO

HALSSNOER

SANTIE

BRACELET

BRACELET

NELLIE

HALSSNOER

MARTHIE

MOLLIE

SOPHIA

CECILIA

STONEHENGE

AMETHYS

BERIL

PARK

RUBY

BANKET

VAN DER WALT

JORDAAN

STANLEY

BANKET

Nelspruit Hospital

▲Shooting Range

PARK

STONEHENGE EXT. 1

PARK

CLARRIE

BETTIE

MARGRIET

MARGRIET

JOHANNA

JOHN VORSTER

IRIS

IRIS

SME

MARIE

ESTHER

ESTHER

To Barberton

R40

To Uitkyk Pass

JOHN VORSTER

Copyright ©Map Studio

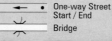

▬▬ Freeway	──── Main Through Route
▬▬ National Route	──── Other Road

Route Numbers

One-way Street Start / End

Bridge

Railway

Station

Other Rail

Built-up Area

Park

Scale 1 : 20 000

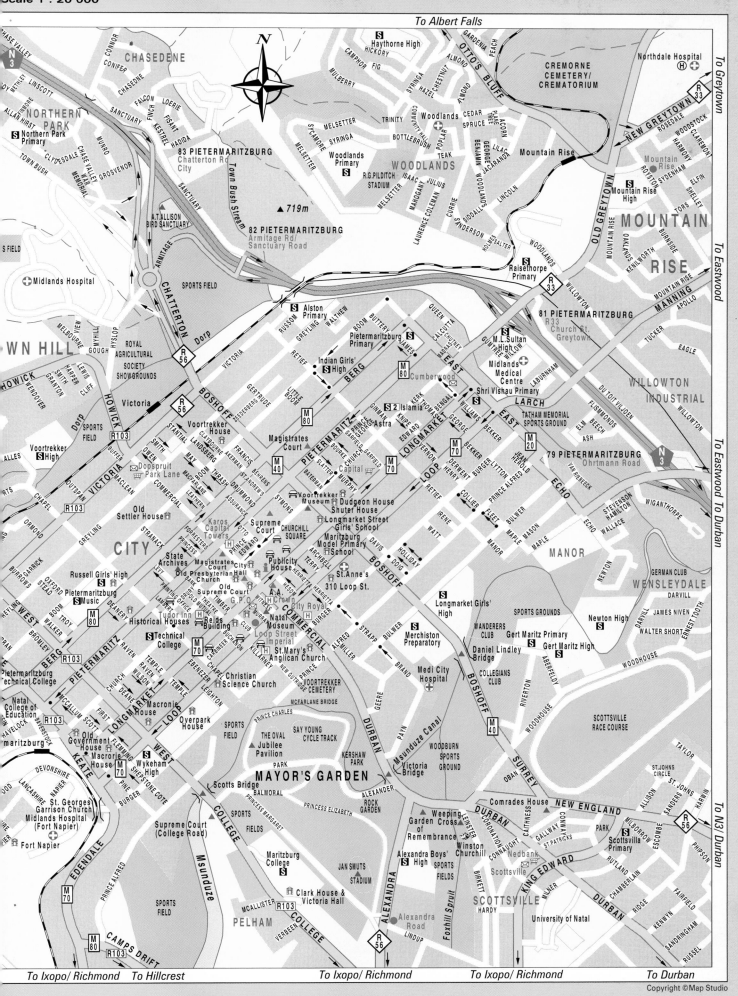

Copyright © Map Studio

Major Airport	Tourist Information Centre	National Monument	Police Station	Recreation Centre	Hospital (24 hour Casualty)	Parking
Airfield	Hotel	Theatre	Community Service	Library	Hospital	Caravan Park
Heliport	Place of Interest	Cinema	Post Office	School	Clinic	Major Shopping Centre

Scale 1 : 20 000

0   200   400

To Seshego · To Dendron

SANDRIVIER

ANNADALE

LADINE

WESTENBURG

INDUSTRIA

SUPERBIA

HOSPITALPARK

EDUANPARK

BENDOR EXT.7

WELGELEGEN

BENDOR

MÔREGLOED

STERPARK

CAPRICORN

FAUNA PARK

To Matlala
To N1/Pretoria
To Pretoria
To N1/Pretoria
To Lydenburg

To Pietersburg Game Reserve · To Flora Park · To Flora Park

	Freeway		Main Through Route		Route Numbers		One-way Street Start / End		Railway		Built-up Ar
	National Route		Other Road				Bridge		Railway Station		Park
									Other Rail		

Scale 1 : 20 000

200 400 600m

KEY TO NUMBERS ON MAP
1. Municipal Offices
2. Brister House
3. JewishPioneer's Memorial Synagogue
4. Market Square,City Hall,Prester John Monument
5. Harbour Board Building(White House)
6. Feather Market Hall
7. Old G.P.O
8. Airways Terminal
9. Little Theatre
10. Atheaneum Building
11. 8 and 9 Bird St.
12. Supreme Court
13. Cora Terrace

ALGOA BAY

To Skoenmakerskop

To Summerstrand

To Walmer   To Humansdorp   To Walmer

Copyright ©Map Studio

Major Airport
Airfield
Heliport

Tourist Information Centre
Hotel
Place of Interest

National Monument
Theatre
Cinema

Police Station
Community Service
Post Office

Recreation Centre
Library
School

Hospital (24 hour Casualty)
Hospital
Clinic

Parking
Caravan Park
Major Shopping Centre

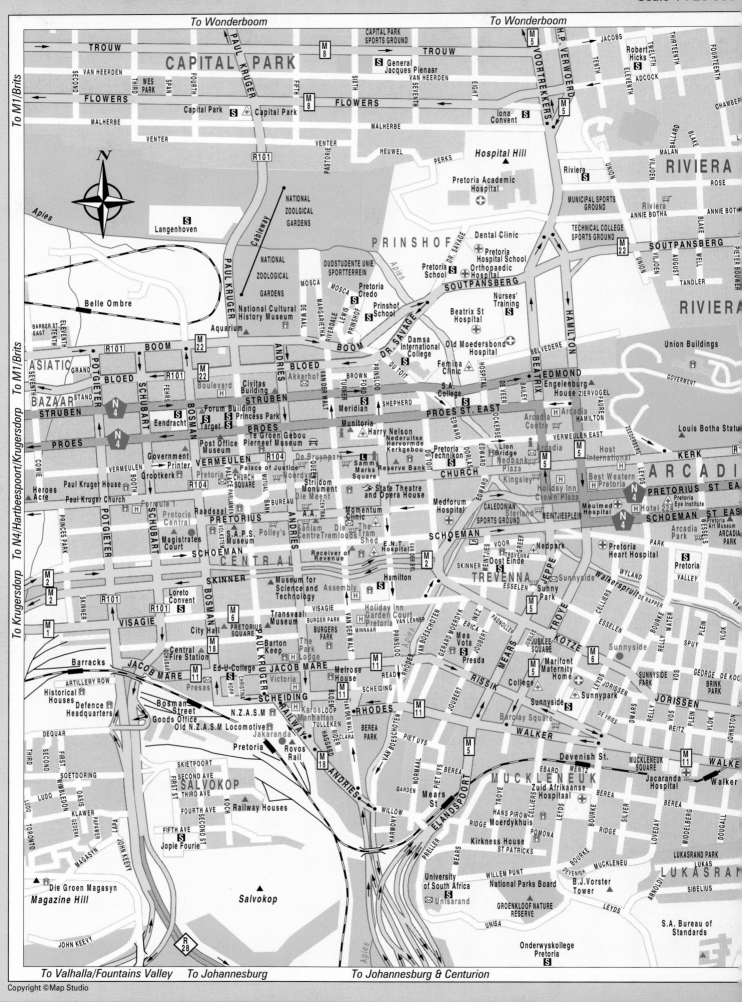

Scale 1 : 20 000

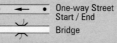

Freeway	Main Through Route	N1 R33 2 Route Numbers
National Route	Other Road	27 R706 M61
		One-way Street Start / End
		Bridge
		Railway
		Station
		Other Rail
		Built-up Area
		Park

Scale 1 : 25 000 000

PAGE 64
BEITBRIDGE TO JOHANNESBURG
PRETORIA TO BLOEMFONTEIN

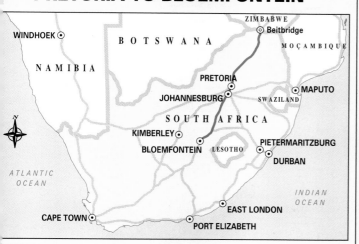

PAGE 65
BLOEMFONTEIN TO CAPE TOWN
BLOEMFONTEIN TO PORT ELIZABETH

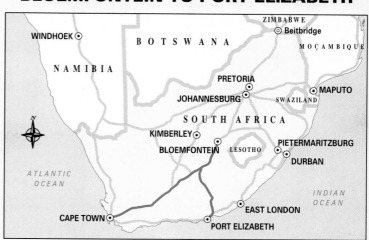

PAGE 66
JOHANNESBURG TO KIMBERLEY
KIMBERLEY TO CAPE TOWN

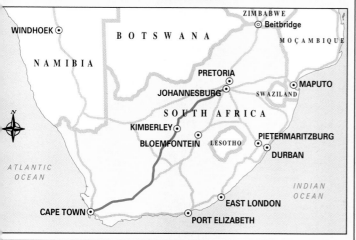

PAGE 67
JOHANNESBURG TO DURBAN
PIETERMARITZBURG TO CAPE TOWN

LEGEND TO STRIP ROUTES

The strip route maps are a representation of features
to be found en route and are not drawn to scale
Kilometre distances are given in black figures,
depending on direction of travel.

tarred — under — untarred construction	Freeway and National Road	● Major City
	Principal Trunk Road	■ Towns on Route
	Main Road	● Other Town
	Secondary Road	✈ Major Airport
N1, R33, R523, T T	Route Numbers	✠ Airfield
	Toll Route and Toll Plaza	⌂ Accommodation
15, 22	Distances in Kilometres	• Place of Interest
	Mountain Passes	★ Historical Site
	Railway	⊣ Border Control
	International & Provincial Boundary	▲ Major Spot Height
	National Park and Nature Reserve	Marsh
	Water Features	Waterfall

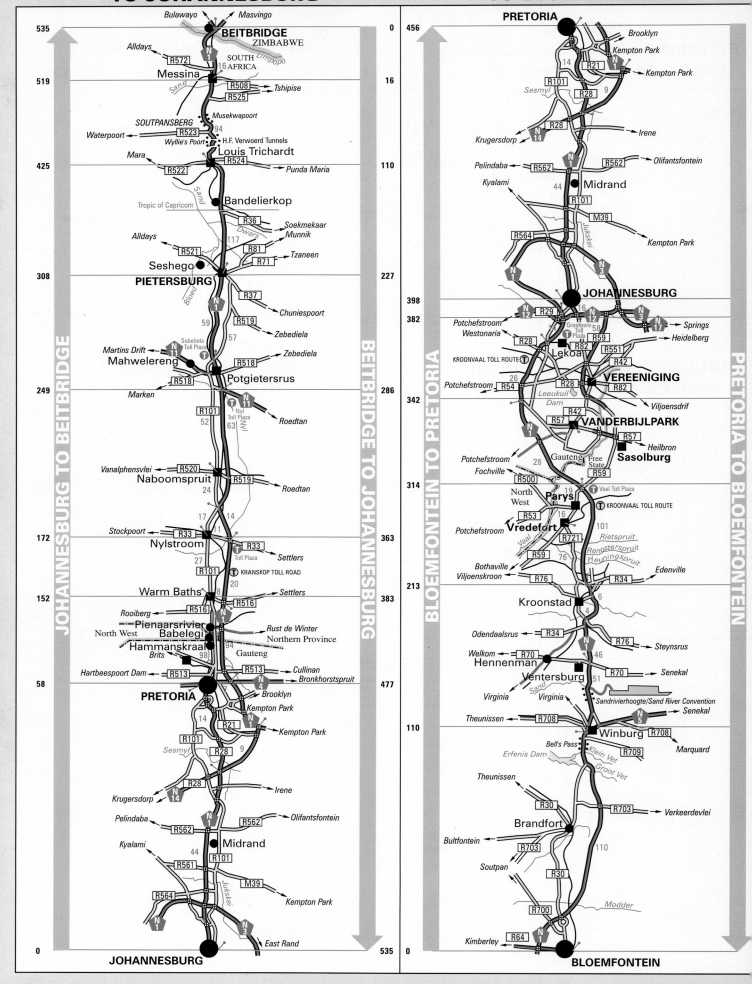

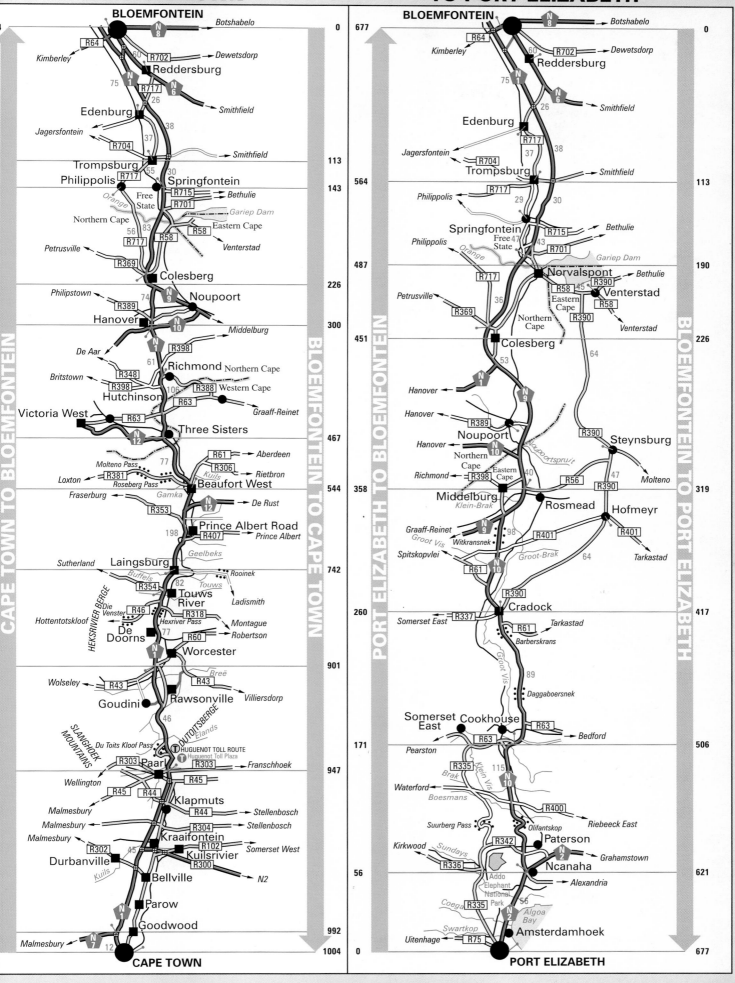

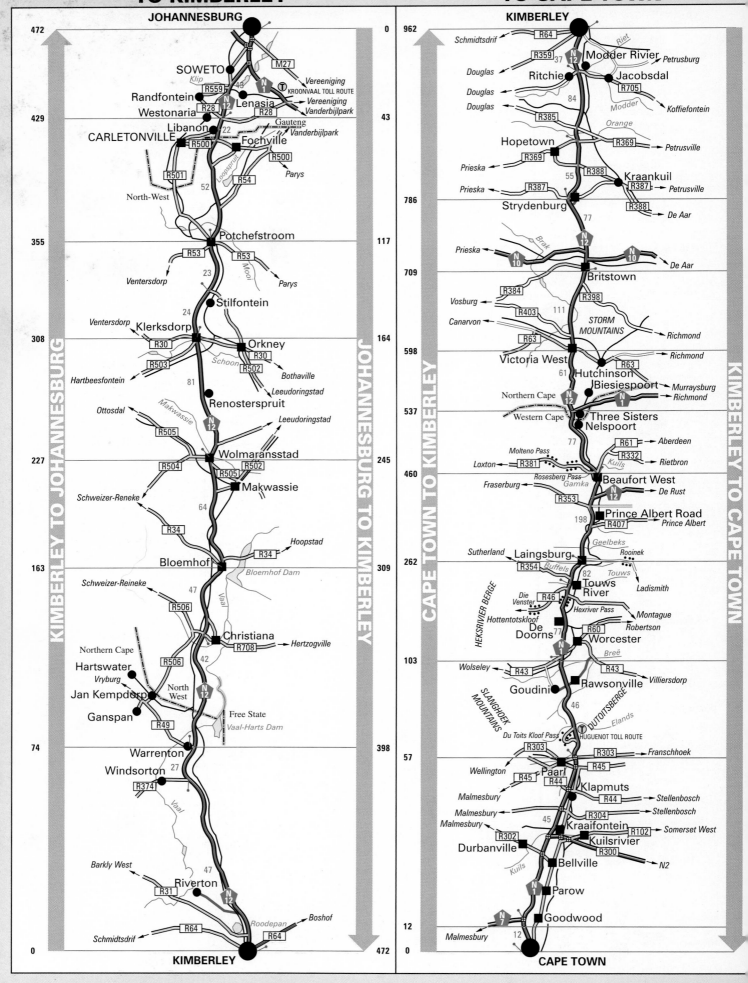

Left column — JOHANNESBURG TO DURBAN

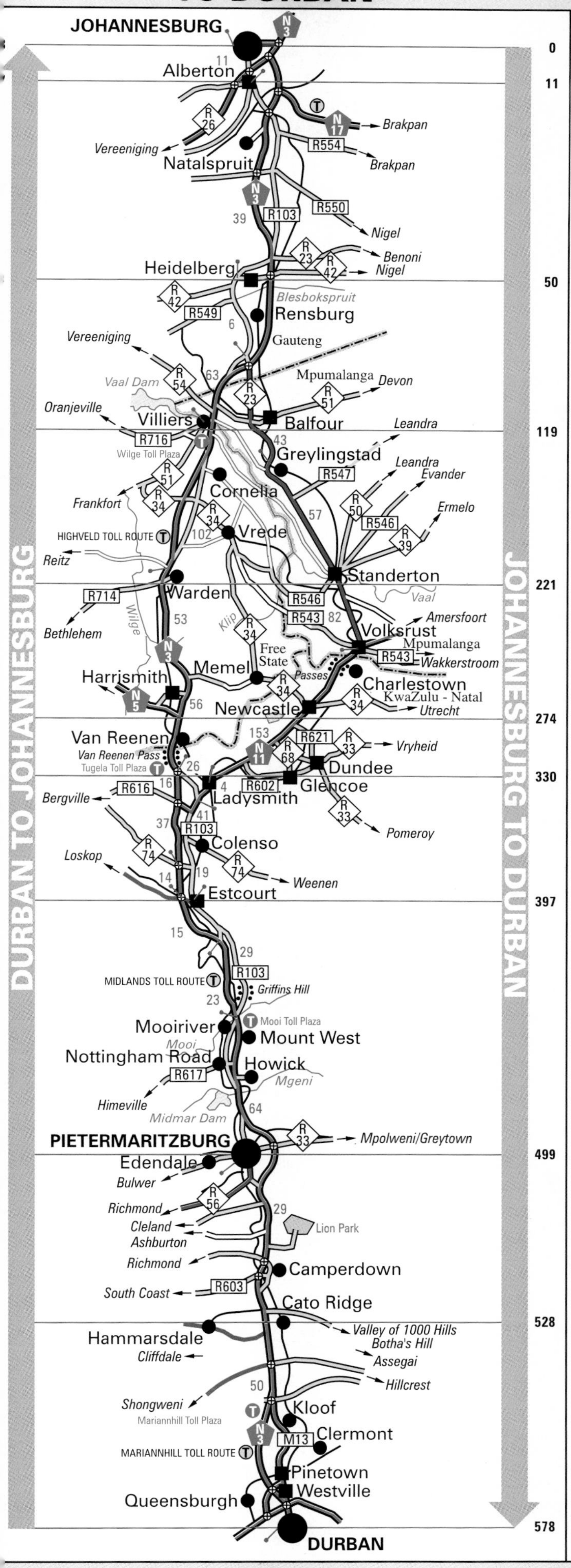

JOHANNESBURG — 0
N3
Alberton — 11 — 11
R26
Brakpan
N17
R554
Vereeniging
Natalspruit
N3
39
R103
R550
Nigel
Benoni
Nigel
Heidelberg — 50
R23 R42
R42
R549
6
Blesbokspruit
Rensburg
Gauteng
Vereeniging
R54 R23
63
Gauteng
Mpumalanga
Devon
Vaal Dam
R51
Oranjeville
Villiers — 119
R716
43
Wilge Toll Plaza
Greylingstad
R547
Leandra
Leandra
Evander
R51 R34
Cornelia
Frankfort
R34
Vrede
57
R50
R546
Ermelo
HIGHVELD TOLL ROUTE
102
R39
Reitz
Warden — 221
R714
R546
Vaal
R543 82
53
Volksrust
Amersfoort
R34
Mpumalanga
Free State
R543
Wakkerstroom
Bethlehem
Klip
Memel
R34
Passes
Charlestown
Harrismith — 899 / 274
N5
34
KwaZulu-Natal
56
Newcastle
Utrecht
Van Reenen
153
R621
R33
Vryheid
Van Reenen Pass
68
Tugela Toll Plaza
26
Dundee — 330
Bergville
R616 16
R602
Glencoe
Ladysmith
4
R33
R103
41
Pomeroy
Loskop
R74
19 R74
Weenen
14
Colenso
Estcourt — 397
15
29
MIDLANDS TOLL ROUTE
R103
Griffins Hill
23
Mooiriver
Mooi Toll Plaza
Mooi
Mount West
Nottingham Road
Howick
R617
Mgeni
Himeville
Midmar Dam
64
PIETERMARITZBURG — 499
R33
Mpolweni/Greytown
Edendale
Bulwer
R56
Richmond
29
Cleland
Lion Park
Ashburton
Richmond
Camperdown
South Coast
R603
Cato Ridge — 528
Hammarsdale
Valley of 1000 Hills
Botha's Hill
Cliffdale
Assegai
50
Hillcrest
Shongweni
Kloof
Mariannhill Toll Plaza
N3
M13
Clermont
MARIANNHILL TOLL ROUTE
Pinetown — 55
Westville
Queensburgh
DURBAN — 578 / 0

Distance markers (centre): 0, 11, 50, 119, 221, 274, 330, 397, 499, 528, 578

DURBAN TO JOHANNESBURG / **JOHANNESBURG TO DURBAN**

Right column — PIETERMARITZBURG TO CAPE TOWN

PIETERMARITZBURG — 1674 / 0
Thornville
38
Durban
Kingsburgh
Richmond
R603
Donnybrook
R56
42
Eastern Cape
R612
Ixopo
R612
Umzimkulu
21 — 101
Franklin
Highflats
Kwazulu-Natal
R617
79
Mzimkulu
Kokstad — 1494 / 180
N2
Kwazulu-Natal
R56
Mtamvuna
Matatiele
Eastern Cape
80
Port Edward
Mount Ayliff
Mount Frere
Tina Hill
Maclear
R396
100
Qumbu
Tsolo
N2
R61
Port St. Johns
R61
Umtata — 1314 / 360
Engcobo
87
Bashee
Coffee Bay
Idutywa
37
Butterworth — 484
Tsomo
Kei Cuttings
Kei
Kei Mouth
Komga
N2
R349
85
111
Stutterheim
Gonubie Mouth
Buffalo
Bisho
EAST LONDON — 595
Braunschweig
27
59
R346
King William's Town
Alice
R63
Peddie
Vis
Fort Beaufort
R67
121
Port Alfred
Cradock
GRAHAMSTOWN — 899 / 775
N10
R72
130
Alexandria
Uitenhage
R75
PORT ELIZABETH — 769 / 905
N2
65
Hankey
R331
Jeffrey's Bay
43
R330
Humansdorp
R332
36
Willowmore
95
INDIAN OCEAN
R62
Joubertina
14
3
Tsitsikamma National Park
TSITSIKAMMA TOLL ROAD
Eastern Cape
Tsitsikamma Toll Plaza
12
19
Uniondale
14
Plettenberg Bay
Western Cape
37
Knysna — 497 / 1177
51
Knysna National Lake Area
Graaff-Reinet
Wilderness National Park
10
George
N9
32
Pacaltsdorp
Oudtshoorn
24
R328
4
Mossel Bay — 400 / 1274
R327
Albertinia
Stilbaai
LANGBERG
Riversdale
R305
Laingsburg
171
Heidelberg
R332
Port Beaufort
Suurbraak
Bredasdorp/Agulhas
Swellendam — 229 / 1445
R60
R317
Ashton
61
Riversonderend
R316
Napier
Villiersdorp
46
Caledon
R43
23
R43
Hermanus
Grabouw
R44
Somerset West
N2
Strand
Kleinmond — 55 / 1619
Bellville
R300
55
Kleinmond
CAPE TOWN — 1674 / 0

Distance markers (right): 0, 101, 180, 360, 484, 595, 775, 905, 1177, 1274, 1445, 1619, 1674

CAPE TOWN TO PIETERMARITZBURG / **PIETERMARITZBURG TO CAPE TOWN**

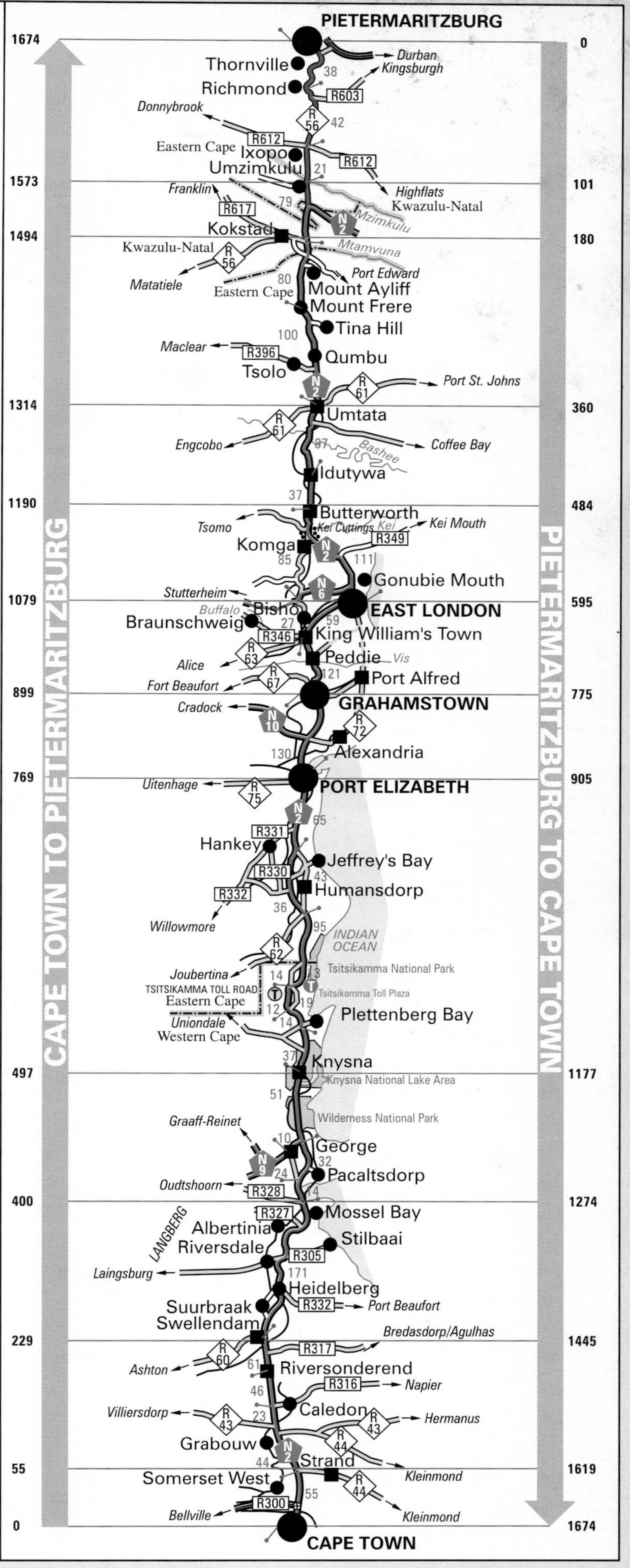

INDEX TO PLACE NAMES

ABBREVIATIONS: E.C. - Eastern Cape N.P. - Northern Province N.W. - North-West
KZN - KwaZulu-Natal W.C. - Western Cape N.C. - Northern Cape Mpum. - Mpumalanga

AALWYNSFONTEIN - DROËRIVIER

INDEX TO PLACE NAMES

DROËVLAKTE - KRANSKOP

INDEX TO PLACE NAMES

Kriel - Olifantshoek

INDEX TO PLACE NAMES

OLYFBERG - TAFELBERG

INDEX TO PLACE NAMES

TAINTON - ZWINGLI

ACKNOWLEDGEMENTS

Photographic Credits

Walter Knirr
Flowers at Clan William (cover), Yellow Billed Hornbill (cover)
Augrabies Falls (Page 10),
Mlanbonya River in the Northern Drakensberg (Page15)
Lion Kill in the Kruger National Park (Page27)

Anthony Bannister Photo Library
The Eye at Kuruman - Lanz von Horsten (Page19)
African Jacana bird in Natal - Nigel Dennis (Page 23),
Cape Point Lighthouse - Hein von Horsten (Page 29),
Port Elizabeth beachfront - George Whittal (Page 39)

Anton van Zyl
Ghost mining town of Kolmanskop (Page 16)

Struik Image Library
East London Beachfront - Hein von Horsten (Page 9)

Cartography
Annette Thomas, Barbara Brightwell, Alicja Schubert,
Gary Coughlan, Sarah Fulcher, Robert Gracie,
Andrew Aikman

Research
Christopher Hosken, Judy Graham

Compilation
Anthony Keeling, Broderick Kupka, Tom Semuguruka

Design
Karien Matthews, Annette Thomas

The publishers acknowledge with thanks the assistance, in the compilation of this Atlas, received from Government Departments, Municipal Authorities, Publicity Departments and many other bodies, both public and private.

Any suggestions regarding amendments or improvements concerning this publication can be addressed post free in South Africa to:- Freepost JHZ 4417, The Research Manager, Map Studio, P O Box 624, Bergvlei, 2012 or e-mail research@mapstudio.co.za